nts

Contents   Page

Author: Melody White.
Artwork, Design, Photographs and Illustrations: Robin Freebairn.

Published in Great Britain by Live The City Publishing.
Production: Labute Group.

Every effort has been made to ensure that the information in this book is correct at the time of going to press. However, details such as telephone numbers, admission fees and opening times are subject to change. The publishers cannot accept any responsibility for consequences arising from the use of this book.

We would be delighted to receive your feedback. Please email: hello@livethecity.com

FSC
Mixed Sources
Product group from well-managed forests and other controlled sources
Cert no. TT-COC-002755
www.fsc.org
© 1996 Forest Stewardship Council

ISBN: 978-0-9562438-0-5   Copyright © 2009 Live The City Ltd.   www.livethecity.com

How to Live The City

Welcome to Cambridge

Thank you for choosing to Live The City. We have designed this unique sightseeing guide to help you make the most of your time in Cambridge.

Inside, you will find three sightseeing trails to complete. Each trail includes fascinating sightseeing information and a series of clues to solve en route. When you've finished exploring, you can complete your Cambridge experience by playing the online quiz based on the clues you've solved. The more you score, the more entries you will earn into our competition prize draw. **Sightseeing with prizes** - what could be better?

Choose the trail which suits you best or complete them all. It's your sightseeing adventure!

For more details about the quiz, see page 64.

CAMBRIDGE ATTRACTS 4.6 MILLION VISITORS EVERY YEAR.

City Highlights Trail

The perfect introduction to Cambridge.

Clare College

Classic sights and hidden treasures await on this fascinating exploration of the city. Pictured are some of the highlights:

 Full Trail   2.5 to 3 hours,
Shorter Trail   2 to 2.5 hours.   .... Let's get started

RIVER CAM

CHESTERTON ROAD

MIDSUMMER COMMON →

KEY

- **S** Start point
- **F** Finish Point
- **1** Clue number and location
- Route
- 👫 Public Toilets
- **P** Car park
- **i** Visitor Information Centre

CASTLE MOUND

CASTLE ROW

ST PETER'S ST

ST PETER'S CHURCH

HONEY HILL

KETTLES YARD FOLK MUSEUM

MARGARET RD

HAYMARKET RD

ALBION ROW

PLEASANT ROW

POUND HILL

LANGLEY ROAD

NORTHAMPTON STREET

CASTLE STREET

CHESTERTON LANE

MAGDALENE COLLEGE

MAGDALENE ST

BRIDGE STREET

QUAYSIDE

THOMPSON'S LANE

ST JOHN'S RD

PARK PARADE

JESUS GREEN

PORTUGAL ST

LOWER PARK ST

PORTUGAL PLACE

ST CLEMENT'S CHURCH

GREAT BRIDGE

BRIDGE OF SIGHS

KITCHEN BRIDGE

ST. JOHN'S COLLEGE

ST. JOHN'S ST

THE ROUND CHURCH

ROUND CH. ST.

PARK ST

JESUS COLLEGE

JESUS LANE

MALCOLM ST

WESCOTT HOUSE

ALL SAINT'S CHURCH

MANOR ST

JESUS LANE

KING STREET

SIDNEY SUSSEX COLLEGE

JESUS LANE

SIDNEY ST

ALL SAINT'S PAS

TRINITY BRIDGE

TRINITY COLLEGE

TRINITY STREET

GREEN STREET

ROSE CRESCENT

MARKET ST

SIDNEY ST

SUSSEX ST

HOBSON STREET

CHRIST'S COLLEGE

CHRIST'S PIECES

BUS STATION

TRINITY HALL

GARRET HOSTEL LANE

GARRET HOSTEL BRIDGE

TRINITY LANE

SENATE HOUSE PAS.

GONVILLE AND CAIUS COLLEGE

CLARE COLLEGE

CLARE BRIDGE

THE BACKS

CLARE COLLEGE

KING'S COLLEGE CHAPEL

KING'S BRIDGE

KING'S COLLEGE

ST. MARY'S ST

GT. ST. MARY'S CH.

KING'S PARADE

ST EDWARDS PAS

PEAS HILL

MARKET SQUARE

MARKET

HOLY TRINITY CHURCH

PETTY CURY

ST. ANDREW THE GREAT CHURCH

ST. ANDREW'S STREET

CHRIST'S LANE

DRUMMER ST

GRAND ARCADE

EMMANUEL STREET

EMMANUEL COLLEGE

WHEELER ST.

CORN EXCHANGE STREET

QUEEN'S ROAD

WEST ROAD

QUEEN'S ROAD

QUEENS' LANE

ST. CATHARINE'S COLLEGE

BENE'T ST

ST BENET'S CHURCH

FREE SCHOOL LANE

CORPUS CHRISTI COLLEGE

OLD CAVENDISH LABORATORY

WHIPPLE MUSEUM

ZOOLOGY MUSEUM

DOWNING STREET

DOWNING STREET

SEDGWICK MUSEUM OF EARTH SCIENCES

DOWNING PLACE

EMMANUEL COLLEGE

PARK TERR

RECENT STREET

MATHEMATICAL BRIDGE

QUEENS' COLLEGE

SILVER STREET

MILL POND

MILL LANE

LT. ST. MARY'S LANE

ST. BOTOLPH'S CHURCH

BOTOLPH LANE

PEMBROKE STREET

MUSEUM OF ARCHAEOLOGY & ANTHROPOLOGY

TENNIS COURT ROAD

PEMBROKE COLLEGE

DOWNING COLLEGE

MUSEUM OF CLASSICAL ARCHAEOLOGY

SIDGWICK AVENUE

DARWIN COLLEGE

GRANTA PLACE

LT. ST. MARY'S CHURCH

TRUMPINGTON ST

PETERHOUSE COLLEGE

FITZWILLIAM ST

TENNIS COURT

FITZWILLIAM MUSEUM

N

BEGIN AT THE CORNER OF PEAS HILL AND BENE'T STREET.

BENE'T ST | ST. BENEDICT'S CHURCH | THE EAGLE PUB

Bene't Street takes its name from the Anglo Saxon Church, St. Benedict's. This area is the medieval heart of the city.

RINGING THE CHANGES

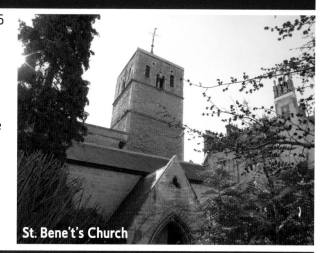
St. Bene't's Church

St. Bene't's church tower dates back to around 1025 and is the oldest building in Cambridgeshire. The ancient churchyard still stands at medieval ground level. The surrounding streets were artificially raised in later years to reduce the flooding risk in the area.

St. Bene't's is thought to be the birthplace of 'change ringing'. Change ringing is the system of sounding bells in an ever changing, rhythmic pattern rather than an actual tune. The man credited with having devised the system was Fabian Steadman, a parish clerk of the church in 1670. A plaque on the wall inside the North tower commemorates this.

THE EAGLE HAS LANDED

The Eagle Pub

The Eagle Pub opposite the church is steeped in history with parts of this former coaching inn date back to the 17th Century. During World War II, the pub became popular with members of the forces based near Cambridge. The ceiling of the back bar is covered with the names of airmen from the RAF and US Air Force, scorched there with cigarette lighters and candles. Look out for the signatures of the crew of the Memphis Belle.

The pub was also popular with scientists working at the nearby Cavendish Laboratory. It was here in February 1953 that James Watson and Francis Crick excitedly announced to other drinkers in the pub that they had discovered the structure of DNA. A plaque outside commemorates this.

1 In their own words, how did Watson and Crick describe their discovery?

NOW CONTINUE TO FREE SCHOOL LANE.

... BEGIN AS THE PEDESTRIAN AREA ENDS ON FREE SCHOOL LANE.

FIRST BOTANIC GARDEN | CAVENDISH LABORATORY

Free School Lane takes its name from the 17th Century school founded here by Dr. Stephen Perse to provide free education for 100 boys from the area.

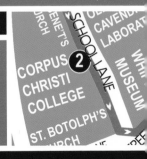

THE ORIGINAL BOTANIC GARDEN

At the end of the pedestrian area, you'll see a small garden behind railings on the left. This is preserved as a memorial to the original Botanic Garden that once stood here. From 1761, the 5-acre site produced plants which were used in the study of botany at the University. In 1874, the Botanic Garden moved to its current site on Trumpington Road. Today, the garden has over 8,000 species of plant within its 40-acre grounds. It is well worth a look if you have time during your visit.

The site of the original Botanic Garden

THE CAVENDISH LABORATORY

Old Cavendish Laboratory Entrance

Walk through the stone archway on your left to enter the Cavendish Laboratory site.

JJ Thompson discovered the electron here in 1897 and Ernest Rutherford, referred to as the 'father of nuclear physics', conducted much of his research on the site. Rutherford was known to be a snappy, short-tempered chap, a characteristic that earned him the nickname 'The Crocodile'. You'll find an engraving of a crocodile on the wall of the Mond Laboratory in his memory. A little further into the site is the Gordon Laboratory. It was here that Watson and Crick completed their research into the structure of DNA. Return to Free School Lane.

2 This clue will drive you up the wall! Opposite JJ's plaque on Free School Lane, if PSB = 1834, what does ST BT P =?

FANCY A DIVERSION?

The Zoology Museum, Sedgwick and Archaeology and Anthropology Museums are all located on Downing Street. Refer to the Museums pages 56-59 for details.

... TURN LEFT ON DOWNING STREET AND CONTINUE TO TENNIS COURT ROAD.

... FROM DOWNING STREET TURN RIGHT INTO TENNIS COURT ROAD.

PEMBROKE COLLEGE | FITZWILLIAM MUSEUM

Tennis Court Road takes its name from the Real Tennis Court that once stood here. The road is lined with University buildings including Pembroke College on the right and Downing College on the left.

PEMBROKE AND DOWNING COLLEGES

embroke is the third oldest college. The college hapel is one of Sir Christopher Wren's earliest works. A statue of William Pitt, the Pembroke graduate who ecame England's youngest Prime Minister, can be ound within the grounds. If you wish to visit the ollege, the entrance can be found on Trumpington treet. Downing College was founded in 1800 as art of the will of Sir George Downing, grandson of he man who built Downing Street in London.

Pembroke College

FITZWILLIAM STREET

Fitzwilliam Street

One of the greatest scientists of all time, Charles Darwin, lived at 22 Fitzwilliam Street between 1836 and 1837. Appropriately, the street is now home to the Leverhulme Centre, dedicated to the study of human evolution.

3 Words from a revolutionary work are displayed somewhere nearby. Specifically, which chapter is featured? The answer is 'clear' to see....

FITZWILLIAM MUSEUM

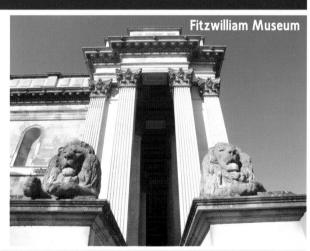

Fitzwilliam Museum

ontinue to Trumpington Street and the Fitzwilliam Museum. Here, you will find collections by artists uch as Titian, Constable, Monet and Picasso as well s antiquities from Ancient Egypt, Greece and Rome. he Museum was established when the 7th Viscount itzwilliam bequeathed his library and art collection to he University in 1816. The collection was originally oused on Free School Lane, but moved to this nagnificent building, designed by architect George asevi, in 1848. Tragically, Basevi was killed in a fall rom one of the towers of Ely Cathedral whilst nspecting repairs. He died in 1845, some three years efore the museum was completed.

... CONTINUE ALONG TRUMPINGTON STREET TOWARDS THE TOWN CENTRE.

✦ ... BEGIN OUTSIDE PETERHOUSE.

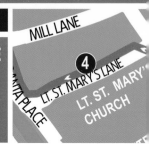

HOBSON'S CONDUIT | PETERHOUSE | LT. ST.MARY'S LANE

Trumpington Street dates back to Anglo Saxon times and leads into King's Parade. A gate to the city once stood at the end of the street beside the 13th Century Church of St. Botolph.

✦ HOBSON'S CONDUIT

The small channels that run along the street are known as 'Hobson's Conduit'. 17th Century townsman Thomas Hobson installed the conduit to carry fresh water into the city. Hobson also ran a livery yard and was famed for lending his horses in a strict rota system. His decision as to which animal was provided was final, coining the phrase "Hobson's Choice", meaning no choice at all.

✦ THE UNIVERSITY'S OLDEST COLLEGE

Peterhouse

Peterhouse is the University's oldest college and was founded on this site in 1284. Hugo de Balsham, the then Bishop of Ely, intended the college to accommodate fourteen 'worthy but impoverished fellows'. Today, Peterhouse has 284 undergraduates, 130 graduate students and 45 fellows, making it the smallest college in the University. Peterhouse is believed to be haunted by the ghost of an 18th Century college bursar. Three exorcisms have been held to banish the ghost, the most recent in 1997.

✦ LITTLE ST. MARY'S CHURCH AND LANE

Godfrey Washington, great uncle of US president George Washington, was once the parish vicar of Little St. Mary's. A plaque inside the church bears his coat of arms which forms the basis of the Stars and Stripes flag. Pretty Little St. Mary's Lane has been inhabited since around 1300 and was once home to the bargemen who made their living transporting grain and coal along the river.

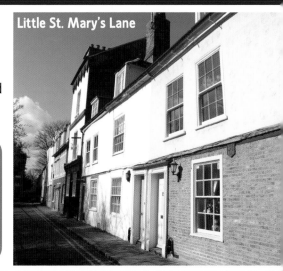
Little St. Mary's Lane

4 Celestial signs may reveal the name of the former inn on Little St. Mary's Lane. What was it called?

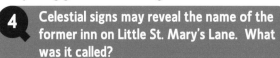

✦ PUNTING ON THE POND

Turn right at the end of Little St. Mary's Lane. The Mill Pond at the end of Granta Place is home to several punting stations. From this point, it is possible to punt along 'The Backs' or out of the city towards Grantchester. For the brave, self hire punting is available although the chauffeured option is far less strenuous!

✦ ... WALK UP LAUNDRESS LANE AND TURN LEFT ON SILVER STREET.

... BEGIN ON SILVER STREET BRIDGE.

QUEENS' COLLEGE | THE MATHEMATICAL BRIDGE

There are two possible explanations as to the origin of the name Silver Street. According to an 18th Century map, the area was home to several silversmiths. Another theory is that the street was once a toll crossing into the town.

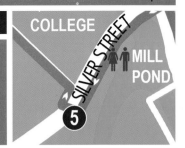

THE ANCHOR PUB

The Anchor Pub has stood in this spot for centuries. During the 1960s, the pub held regular jazz nights earning the name The Riverside Jazz Bar. One of the regulars at the time was a student called Keith Barrett. He particularly admired the house band's drummer, named Sid. Keith adopted the nickname Little Syd, spelt with a 'Y' to avoid confusion. "Syd" went on to form legendary rock band Pink Floyd.

The Anchor Pub

THE BRIDGE OF LIES!

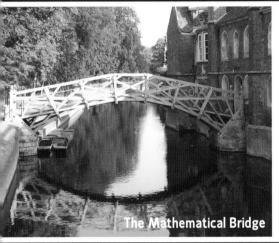

The Mathematical Bridge

Queens' College is named after its two patronesses, Margaret of Anjou (wife of Henry VI) and Elizabeth Woodville (wife of Edward IV).

The college's most famous landmark is the Mathematical Bridge visible from Silver Street. The bridge, dating back to 1749, is the subject of two Cambridge myths. Firstly, it is said to have been built without nails or bolts, with these only being added when the bridge was taken down by students who were unable to put it back together again. Secondly, it is rumoured that the bridge was designed by Sir Isaac Newton. Sadly neither story is true. The bridge was built by James Essex to a design by William Etheridge.

DARWIN COLLEGE

Darwin College stands at the end of Silver Street. Darwin is a postgraduate college and was founded in 1964. The college takes its name from descendants of Charles Darwin who owned the land it is built on.

5 Charles' grandaughter favoured the arts. Find a record outside the college of her particular achievements.

Darwin College from Laundress Green

... FOLLOW THE SANDSTONE PATHWAY ALONG 'THE BACKS' PARALLEL TO QUEEN'S ROAD.

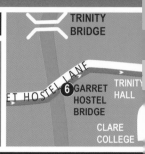

TRINITY
BRIDGE

...CONTINUE WALKING, PASSING THE ICONIC VIEW OF KING'S COLLEGE.

THE BACKS | CLARE COLLEGE | CLARE BRIDGE

'The Backs' are so called as, from this point, only the backs of the colleges are visible. Cattle still graze on the meadowland beside the river, adding to the charm of the picture postcard view of King's College Chapel.

CLARE COLLEGE

Clare College is the second oldest in the University. It was first founded in 1326 as 'University Hall' and re-founded in 1338 by Lady Elizabeth de Clare, granddaughter of King Edward I. Elizabeth's early life was filled with tragedy. Before her 28th birthday, she had been widowed three times. After the death of her third husband, she devoted herself and her considerable fortune to charitable works, including the re-founding of Clare College. For the remainder of her life, Elizabeth wore a black mourning band decorated with golden tears in memory of her former husbands. The golden tears on a black band are represented on the college coat of arms which can be found on the iron gate to the college grounds.

Clare's grounds span both sides of Queen's Road. Across the road, you should be able to see the large sculpture of a double helix within the college grounds. The sculpture is a tribute to James Watson who was a graduate student at Clare at the time he co-discovered the structure of DNA.

Clare College from Trinity Lane

THE ARCHITECT'S REVENGE

Clare Bridge

Continue to Garret Hostel Bridge and look south towards Clare Bridge, the oldest surviving bridge in the city. One of the fourteen stone balls which decorate the bridge has a segment missing. Legend has it that the bridge's architect left this mark as revenge when the college refused to pay him in full! There have been at least eight former bridges crossing the river at Garret Hostel Lane. This one dates back to 1960.

6 Use your TRUSTED intuition to discover who designed Garret Hostel Bridge. The Jerwood Library may be of assistance.

...CONTINUE TO THE END OF GARRET HOSTEL LANE, TURNING RIGHT ON TRINITY LANE.

...BEGIN AT THE START OF SENATE HOUSE PASSAGE.

THE SENATE HOUSE | GONVILLE AND CAIUS COLLLEGE

At this point, you may wish to visit King's College Chapel which is accessed via Trinity Lane. You will find a section about the chapel on pages 54 and 55.

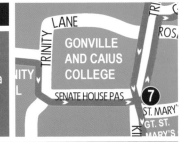

CEREMONIES AND STUDENT ANTICS

To the right of Senate House Passage is the Senate House, built by James Gibbs between 1722 and 1730. This is the ceremonial centre of the University and is where students receive their degrees.

In a famous prank, on the night of 7th June 1958, engineering students from neighbouring Gonville & Caius College hoisted an Austin Seven van onto the roof of the Senate House. It was a feat of engineering ingenuity and it took college officials several days and a large crane to remove the van!

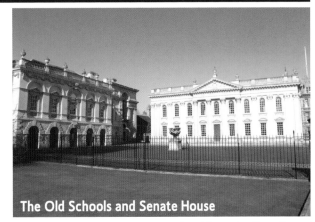

The Old Schools and Senate House

GONVILLE AND CAIUS COLLEGE

Gonville And Caius

Gonville and Caius College was first founded in 1348 by Norfolk priest Edmund Gonville. Gonville's motivation was to provide education for trainee priests after clergy numbers were depleted following the Black Death. Some 200 years later, Dr. John Caius, the second founder, brought money and a new style to the college, introducing architecture based on that he had seen whilst studying in Italy. In fact, Caius was so enamoured with all things Italian that he even changed his name from the English spelling, Keys, to its Latin equivalent.

There are three main gates to the three sided Caius Court. Each gate symbolises a different stage in the path of learning. Students enter through the Gate of Humility, pass through the Gate of Virtue and leave the college, upon graduation, via the Gate of Honour.

7 On Trinity Street, find the house of words. What is its notable claim?

...TURN LEFT ALONG TRINITY STREET AND THEN SECOND RIGHT INTO GREEN STREET.

... CONTINUE ALONG GREEN STREET.

GREEN STREET | SIDNEY SUSSEX COLLLEGE

This pretty street has some interesting boutique shops to explore. The cobbles on the street were restored in 1999.

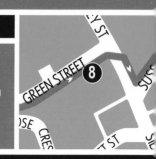

WHAT'S IN A NAME?

According to local legend, Green Street takes its name from the time of the plague, when both ends of the street were bricked up, trapping the sick inhabitants inside to halt the spread of the disease. When the walls were eventually removed, grass had grown between the cobbles of the street. Although this gruesome practice did happen in some cities and although Cambridge did suffer greatly during the plague (many victims were buried in mass graves beneath nearby Midsummer Common), this story is probably no more than macabre folklore. It is more likely that the street is named after the man who owned the land it was built upon, which is much less interesting!

8 Which 'Generally Artistic' father and son look down from the 'borders' of Green Street?

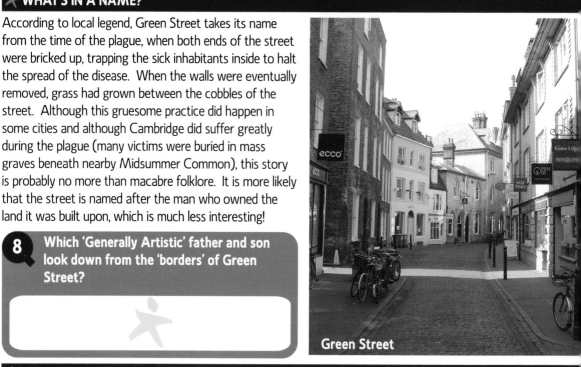

Green Street

SIDNEY'S GRUESOME SECRET

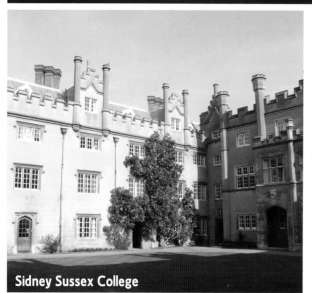

Sidney Sussex College

At the end of Green Street stands Sidney Sussex College. Sidney (as it commonly known) was founded in 1596 by Lady Frances Sidney, Countess o Sussex. Oliver Cromwell was one of the college's first students although he never graduated, leaving after just one year following the death of his father.

Cromwell died of natural causes in 1658 and was buried with great ceremony in Westminster Abbey. In 1661, after the monarchy had been restored, Cromwell's body was exhumed and posthumously 'executed'. His severed head was displayed on an iron stake outside The Abbey until 1685. After this, the head changed hands several times until it finally made its way to the college in 1960. It is now buried in a secret location somewhere within the college chapel.

... FOR THE SHORTER TRAIL SKIP TO PAGE 17. FOR THE LONGER TRAIL READ ON.

🏃... **TURN RIGHT THEN LEFT DOWN SUSSEX STREET TO KING STREET.**

THE KING STREET RUN | CAMBRIDGE'S SMALLEST PUB.

This street is notorious in Cambridge for drunken antics! In fact, one of the pubs on the street is named in honour of a student drinking game - The King Street Run.

🏃 A VERY CAMBRIDGE PUB CRAWL

The King Street Run first came about in the winter of 1955/6. A group of students from St. John's were discussing how many pubs it was possible to drink in without having to relieve oneself. To settle the argument, the students agreed to investigate this the following night in King Street. The aim was to drink a pint of beer in each of the eight pubs without visiting the facilities! Half the students failed to turn up, but three off duty Royal Navy sailors offered to join in. Amazingly, the three sailors and most of the students accomplished the feat! The race has now become a student tradition, with a specially designed tie awarded to those who complete the 'run' in under an hour. Since there are now only five pubs on King Street, and the run requires drinking eight pints, the last three are visited twice.

Pub Sign on King Street

🏃 GOOD THINGS COME IN SMALL PACKAGES

St. Radegund Pub

The St. Radegund Pub, at the end of King Street closest to Midsummer Common, is the smallest pub in Cambridge. The pub has its own running club, the Hash House Harriers - 'The drinking club with a running problem'.

The pub has several 'specials' nights and Friday is Vera Lynn Night (Vera Lynn — Gin). To celebrate the start of the weekend, double G&Ts are served up for the price of a single between 5.30 and 7.30pm. The end of 'Vera time' is signalled by the soulful sound of 'We'll meet again' playing on the juke box!

9 Elsewhere on King Street, find a pub's dedication to 'splendid fellows'. What do these fellows remain?

🏃... **HEAD TO JESUS LANE VIA MANOR STREET.**

...BEGIN AT ALL SAINTS CHURCH ON JESUS LANE.

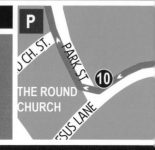

ALL SAINTS CHURCH | JESUS COLLEGE

Recent excavations in the Jesus Lane area have uncovered Bronze Age and Iron Age settlement remains and the presence of a Roman cemetery beneath the houses on Malcolm Street.

ALL SAINTS CHURCH

All Saints was completed in 1870. Its striking interior is typical of the Arts and Crafts Movement of the time. William Morris, leading designer of the movement, created much of the wall decoration and stained glass windows.

The church is not used for worship anymore but is preserved as a visitor attraction.

Tower details on All Saints Church

JESUS COLLEGE

Jesus College

Jesus College was founded in 1496 by John Alcock, Bishop of Ely, on the site of the former 12th Century Benedictine nunnery of St Radegund. When Bishop Alcock first visited the nunnery, he found it virtually deserted, with only two nuns remaining. He persuaded Henry VII to allow him to transform the site into a college. Many of the original nunnery buildings remain to this day including the college chapel which was originally the nuns' church. The chapel is the oldest building still in use within the entire University. Bishop Alcock's symbol, the black cockerel, forms the basis of the college coat of arms.

One of the most famous graduates of the college was Thomas Cranmer who began his studies here aged just 14. Cranmer went on to become the first Protestant Archbishop of Canterbury and was burned at the stake in 1556 during the reign of Mary Tudor.

Continue to the corner of Park Street.

10 Which college is mentioned in miniature nearby?

...TURN RIGHT INTO PARK STREET.

🏃... **TURN LEFT INTO PORTUGAL PLACE NEXT TO THE MAYPOLE PUB.**

PORTUGAL PLACE | JESUS GREEN | THE GREAT BRIDGE

Portugal Place earned its name from the huge quantities of Port which were once transported into Cambridge on barges. The area around Portugal Place is where the drink was stored in warehouses. Most of the Port was destined for the fellows of the colleges.

🏃 THE HAWKS CLUB

Number 18, Portugal Place is home to the Hawks Club. The Hawks serves the entire University, but membership to the elite sporting club is by election only. Generally only those who have a 'Blue' can join. A 'Blue' is an award earned when the sportsman or woman has competed against Oxford in their particular sport. Former members include England cricketer Mike Atherton and actor Hugh Laurie, who in 1980, participated in the University Boat Race.

11 On Portugal Place, find the former home of this poetic and philosophical Trinity graduate. With which country is he associated with?

Portugal Place

🏃 A WALK IN THE PARK?

Jesus Green

If you have time, make a short detour for a relaxing stroll in Jesus Green, one of the city's many pretty parks.

Cambridge is a very green city, with several similar spaces. Jesus Green is home to the annual beer festival in May and the summer Comedy Festival. It is also the site of one of the country's longest outdoor swimming pools.

🏃 BRIDGE OVER THE RIVER CAM

Go to Bridge Street and turn right towards the river. There has been a bridge crossing the river in this spot for over a thousand years. In fact, the city takes its name from this point — 'Bridge' over the River 'Cam'. Periodically, the current bridge, built in 1823, undergoes repairs for damage caused by the heavy traffic crossing the river. As a result of attempts to reduce this damage, only buses and taxis can now access the street.

The Great Bridge

🏃... **CROSS THE GREAT BRIDGE AND CONTINUE TO THE CROSSROADS ON CHESTERTON LANE.**

... CROSS CHESTERTON LANE AND WALK UP CASTLE STREET.

CAMBRIDGE CASTLE | KETTLE'S YARD | ST. PETER'S CHURCH

You are now entering the most hilly part of Cambridge. Don't worry though, you won't find the gradient too strenuous! The Castle Pub stands halfway up the hill just before the entrance to the site of the former Cambridge castle.

CAMBRIDGE CASTLE

Today, nothing remains of the castle except the mound it once stood upon. The small climb to the top is worth the effort for the lovely view across the whole of Cambridge. The first castle was built in 1068 by the conquering Normans and provided an excellent lookout across the surrounding area. In the 13th Century, a stone castle replaced the original timber structure and this remained, for many years as a prison, until the 19th Century. In the mid 1800s, the building ceased to be occupied and much of the stone from the ruins was used in the construction of University buildings. Shire Hall, which faces the castle, is the administrative headquarters of the county.

Castle Mound

ST PETER'S CHURCH

St. Peter's Church

Return to Castle Street and begin your descent. On your right is pretty little St. Peter's Church, which was built in 1781 on the site of an earlier church dating back to the 11th Century. A Roman temple is thought to have originally stood here.

The church is open to visitors most of the time but if closed, a key can be borrowed from nearby Kettle's Yard Gallery.

KETTLE'S YARD

Kettle's Yard Gallery and the Cambridge Folk Museum stand at the bottom of Castle Street. The Folk Museum, a social history museum, houses a fascinating collection of artefacts depicting centuries of life in the local area. Kettle's Yard houses art collections and exhibitions.

12 What is 14 miles, 4 furlongs away from this point?

Kettle's Yard

... RETURN TO MAGDALENE STREET.

... HEAD TO MAGDALENE COLLEGE ON MAGDALENE STREET.

MAGDALENE COLLEGE | PEPYS LIBRARY | THE PICKEREL

In Cambridge, Magdalene College and Street are pronounced 'Maudlin'. This unusual pronunciation may have arisen as a tribute to the college founder, Sir Thomas Audley.

13
GREAT BRIDGE

MAGDALENE COLLEGE

Magdalene began life in 1428 as a hostel for Benedictine monks. In 1542, under the guidance of Sir Thomas Audley, Lord Chancellor to Henry VIII, the College of St. Mary Magdalene was founded on the site.

Magdalene is considered a very traditional establishment and was the last all male college in either Cambridge or Oxford University. Women were finally admitted for the first time in 1988 when a number of the male undergraduates and fellows wore black armbands in protest against the move.

Magdalene College from Quayside

SAMUEL PEPYS

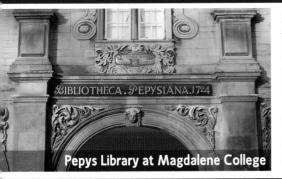

Pepys Library at Magdalene College

Magdalene is home to the Pepys Library, bequeathed by the 17th Century diarist and perhaps the most famous graduate of the college, Samuel Pepys. In line with Pepys' wishes, no books can be taken from nor added to the 3,000 strong collection.

When open, the grounds of the college are free to visit, although the Pepys Library can only be viewed at certain times. Ask at the Porter's Lodge for details.

CAMBRIDGE'S OLDEST PUB

The Pickerel Pub stands opposite Magdalene College. At over 600 years old, the pub is believed to be the oldest in the city and has, in its time, been a brothel, a gin palace and an opium den! No doubt Pepys frequented the pub during his time at the college.

13 Another inn once stood close to The Pickerel. Can you 'unlock' its name with help from a nearby yard?

The Pickerel Inn

... CONTINUE ALONG BRIDGE STREET TO THE ROUND CHURCH.

🏃... HEAD TOWARDS THE ROUND CHURCH ON BRIDGE STREET.

THE ROUND CHURCH | CAMBRIDGE UNION SOCIETY.

The Tudor buildings which line Bridge Street are the few which escaped demolition during the expansion of St. John's College. Most of these now house bars and restaurants, making this a popular place to eat and drink.

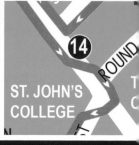

ST. JOHN'S COLLEGE

🏃 THE ROUND CHURCH

14 Before you get to the church, find the pub with the theological sounding name. Who ran the Cock and Magpie in 1874?

The 'Round Church' or Holy Sepulchre to use its correct name is one of only four surviving round churches in England and dates back to around 1130. The church was founded by the Fraternity of the Holy Sepulchre. Very little is known about the Fraternity but it is thought that they had links to the Crusades. The church is built to a design based on the original Church of the Holy Sepulchre in Jerusalem. Much of the building was authentically restored in the mid 19th Century.

The Round Church

🏃 THE ART OF THE DEBATING

Cambridge Union Society

The small passageway to the right of the church leads to the Cambridge Union Society Building. The Union Society was founded in 1815 supposedly as a result of a drunken brawl between several college debating societies. Originally, the society 'for gentlemen only' was extremely elitist. For many years, debates were held in the back rooms of local pubs until, finally, in 1866, this building was opened. Today, the society is open to all University members. The Union has welcomed countless world leaders including President Roosevelt, Churchill, the Dalai Llama and Archbishop Desmond Tutu. During WWII, the Chamber was used by Field Marshall Montgomery to discuss plans for the D-Day Landings. In 1999, the Union held the 'Kosovo Forum' which saw representatives from the Kosovo Liberation Army and the Serbian Government come together for the first time. It can truly be said that history has been, and continues to be, made here.

🏃... MOVE ON TO SAINT JOHN'S STREET.

✦... START TO WALK DOWN SAINT JOHN'S STREET.

ST. JOHN'S COLLEGE

You will notice a number of brass flowers set in the pavement near the corner of Saint John's Street. These were created in 2001 by artist Michael Fairfax. The flowers are daisies, or in French, 'margeurites' and relate to the founder of St. John's College — Lady Margaret Beaufort.

ST. JOHN'S COLLEGE

St. John's was founded posthumously by Lady Margaret Beaufort (mother of King Henry VII) in 1511 upon the site of a 13th Century hospital run by the monks of St. John. Originally intended to specialise in the study of liberal arts and theology, the college today has become a centre of excellence in mathematics, humanities, medicine, and sciences. St. John's alumni include the poet William Wordsworth and abolishionist, William Wilberforce.

15 The green iron gates of St. John's reveal the French motto of the college. This is linked to a flower shown on the main gate. Which flower?

St. John's College

MAJESTIC ARCHITECTURE

St. John's College New Court

St. John's has many striking architectural features including the Bridge of Sighs, modelled on the bridge in Venice, and the Gothic New Court, which due to its flamboyant design is known affectionately as 'The Wedding Cake'. Also within the grounds is the School of Pythagoras which is much older that the college itself and dates back to 1200. The red brick Gate Tower on Saint John's Street is decorated with a statue of St. John above Lady Margaret's coat of arms which is supported by 'yales'. These mythical creatures have goats' heads, antelopes' bodies and elephants' tails.

THE BOAT RACE

The annual University Boat Race began when St. John's Lady Margaret Boat Club (the oldest on the river) challenged Oxford to a race in 1829. Oxford won. Oarsmen of the LMBC wear bright scarlet jackets and these were the origin for the word 'blazer', now used to describe sports jackets.

An 'eight' on the River Cam

✦... CONTINUE ALONG TRINITY STREET.

⋆ ... GO TO THE GREAT GATE OF TRINITY COLLEGE.

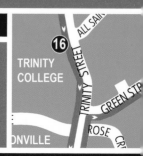

TRINITY COLLEGE

Trinity College is the largest and wealthiest of all the Cambridge Colleges. Trinity alumni include an incredible 32 Nobel prize winners (University members hold 82 in total) and among many others include Sir Isaac Newton, Lord Byron, Tennyson and Sir Francis Bacon.

⋆ THE GREAT GATE

Look closely at the statue of Henry VIII situated at first floor level on the Great Gate. Henry should be holding a sceptre in his right hand. Instead, as a result of a student prank in the late 1800s, he holds something else! The six small shields represent the sons of Edward III. He was founder of King's Hall, an earlier college on this site. The blank shield is for The Earl of Hatfield who died in infancy.

The Great Gate

> **16** Take five steps back from the centre of Trinity's Great Gate. 'Initially' what do you notice? Eyes down!

⋆ THE GREAT COURT RUN

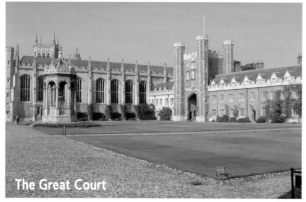

The Great Court

The Great Court beyond the main entrance to the college is the site of the race which inspired the film, Chariots of Fire.

In the Great Court Run, students attempt to run around the circumference of the court within the time it takes the college clock to strike noon. This equates to a distance of 367 metres in less than 43 seconds. In 2007, undergraduate Sam Dobin became only the third person ever to achieve this.

⋆ THE WREN LIBRARY

Trinity's famous Wren Library, designed by Sir Christopher Wren, was completed in 1684. The library is packed full of historically important books including several early editions of Shakespeare's works, a number of Sir Isaac Newton's own collection and the original manuscript of AA Milne's 'Winnie The Pooh'. Both AA and his son Christopher Robin were Trinity graduates. Ask for visiting details at the main gate.

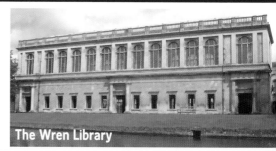

The Wren Library

⋆ ... CONTINUE ALONG TRINITY STREET TO GREAT ST. MARY'S CHURCH.

✦... GO TO GREAT ST. MARY'S CHURCH.

GREAT ST. MARY'S CHURCH

Great St. Mary's was built in the late 15th Century on the site of a church believed to date back to 1205. For fantastic views across the city and beyond, why not climb the 123 steps to the top of the church tower?

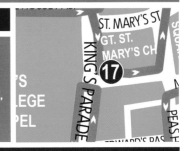

✦ A CHURCH FOR TOWN AND GOWN

Great St. Mary's is both a parish church and the University Church. As the University Church, degree ceremonies were held here until the Senate House was built in 1730. According to University rules, all undergraduates must live within 3 miles of the church. Unusually, Great St Mary's has two church organs, one bought by the University in 1697, and a parish organ dating back to 1869. On rare occasions, the two are played together. Regular concerts and events for both the University and town are held in the church.

Great St. Mary's Church

✦ REFORMATION

One of the two church organs

During the English Reformation, leading philosophers would deliver speeches from Great St. Mary's. One such man, Martin Bucer, was buried in the church when he died in 1551. When Mary Tudor (Bloody Mary) came to the throne six years later, she had Bucer's body exhumed and burnt in the Market Square. When Elizabeth I succeeded to the throne, she had the dust from the site of his execution placed back inside the church.

✦ A FAMILIAR TUNE THAT RINGS A BELL

The 'Westminster Chimes' associated with Big Ben in London are more correctly called the 'Cambridge Chimes'. The sequence, now famous throughout the world, was first rung in 1793 from the clock above the Senate Hill entrance to Great St. Mary's. The Palace of Westminster did not adopt the chimes until the mid 19th Century.

17 Find William beneath the 'Cambridge Chimes'. What is he remembered for?

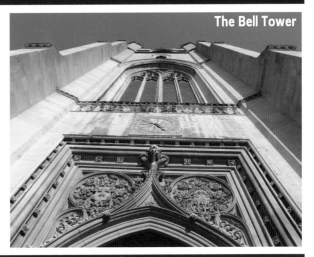
The Bell Tower

✦... MAKE YOUR WAY TO THE MARKET SQUARE.

... BEGIN ON THE MARKET SQUARE.

MARKET SQUARE | THE GUILDHALL

Prior to the great fire of 1849, the area surrounding Great St. Mary's was L-shaped and populated with houses. When these burnt down, the rectangular space, now known as Market Square, was created.

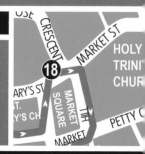

THE MARKET SQUARE

Over the centuries, this site has witnessed 'Town versus Gown' riots between locals and students, the ceremonious burning of Martin Luther's works and countless political protests. It remains the site of political demonstrations to this day. The small ornamental fountain in the centre of the market place was once the site of Hobson's Conduit (now located on Lensfield Road). The railings around the Conduit were used to chain up criminals condemned to a public whipping.

On Sundays, a farmers market is held here and a whole host of locally produced treats can be sampled.

18 Go to the street containing the name of an English flower. What is the subject of Calverley's poem?

The Market Square from Gt. St. Mary's Church

THE GUILDHALL

The Guildhall

The imposing Guildhall was built in 1937, although a town hall has existed on this site since medieval times. The original building was given to the town by Henry III in around 1220. The building was first used to house the town jail until, some 50 years later, it became the site of the Town Hall. Originally the Guildhall stood on stilts, with market stalls operating from the space beneath.

Today, the Guildhall contains the Mayor's Chambers and the offices of many city council departments. Until 2004, the Cambridge Crown Court was also located here.

Despite not having a cathedral, Cambridge was granted city status in 1951 by King George VI.

... CONTINUE TO PEAS HILL.

...BEGIN ON PEAS HILL.

PEAS HILL | THE ARTS THEATRE | ST. EDWARD'S PASSAGE

As a famously flat city, Cambridge has a surprising number of 'Hills' in its street names. These originate from the very earliest recorded settlement in the area, when the first town was founded on the site of several small hills.

PEAS HILL

The different prefixes to 'Hill' relate to the goods that were once traded or activities which took place here. Peas Hill was the site of a fish market and takes its name from the Latin word for fish - piscaria.

Elsewhere in the city there is a Honey Hill, Senate House Hill, Market Hill, Castle Hill and a Pound Hill.

Peas Hill

THE ARTS THEATRE

Cambridge Arts Theatre

CAMBRIDGE ARTS THEATRE

The Arts Theatre was bequeathed to the city by the Cambridge born economist and King's graduate, John Maynard Keynes. Keynes was part of the fashionable 'Bloomsbury Set' during the early 1900s and was a contemporary of Virginia Woolf and Bertrand Russell. For many years, the Cambridge University Footlights staged their annual review at The Arts. The Footlights has provided a platform for actors, comedians and entertainers for over 120 years. Famous former members include Peter Cook, John Cleese, Stephen Fry, Emma Thompson and HRH Prince Edward.

19 Keynes had many strings to his bow. The Arts reveals them all. What were they?

ST. EDWARD'S PASSAGE

The Haunted Bookshop is said to be inhabited by the ghost of an attractive, fair haired woman. There have been several sightings since the first in 1989. When she appears, the air is filled with the smell of violets. The narrow passageway has existed since at least the early 16th Century and is a good example of how cramped Medieval Cambridge must have been.

St. Edward's Passage

...CONTINUE TO KING'S PARADE.

... BEGIN OUTSIDE THE ENTRANCE TO KING'S COLLEGE.

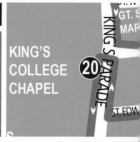

KING'S COLLEGE | CHRONOPHAGE

King's Parade was once the main thoroughfare of the city and was lined with shops and houses on both sides. The street is now dominated by magnificent King's College and the Chapel (more information about the Chapel can be found on pages 54 and 55).

KING'S COLLEGE CHAPEL **20**

KING'S COLLEGE

King's was founded in 1441 by King Henry VI. Due to financial constraints and the disruption of the English Civil War, it took a further 100 years to finish the college as it appears today. During this time, both Henry VII and VIII played a part in its completion.

Originally, the college was to provide education for boys schooled at Eton. In fact, this tradition remained until the first non-Eton educated students were admitted in 1865. Perhaps it is due to these elitist beginnings that King's is now known for admitting one of the highest proportions of state educated students within the University.

Just outside the Neo-Gothic Gatehouse of King's stands a classic British icon in the form of a 19th Century hexagonal postbox bearing the initials VR, Victoria Regina. This is one of the oldest surviving post boxes in the country. It is pictured on the front cover of this guide.

20 Watch your step as you pass the Chapel on King's Parade. Which unlikely phrase do you find?

King's College Chapel

CHRONOPHAGE - THE CORPUS CLOCK

Chronophage

Your trail ends at Cambridge's newest landmark, the Corpus Christi clock at the corner of Bene't Street.

The giant grasshopper which sits on top of the clock is nicknamed 'Chronophage' meaning 'time-eater'. The magnificent clock, designed by Corpus graduate John C Taylor cost £1m and was unveiled by Professor Stephen Hawking in September 2008. This crowd pleasing time piece looks set to become one of the city's most popular and enduring landmarks.

... CONGRATULATIONS, YOU'VE FINISHED! FOR HOW TO PLAY THE QUIZ GO TO PAGE 64.

Punting Trail
Discover the beautiful 'Backs'.

HAT TRICK

MENAGE

LITTLE KITTEN

DIABOLUS IN MUSICA

MILE ISLAND

CHEER

Punts at Trinity College

We have written this trail starting from the Mill Pond end of The Backs. However you can start from any point on the map depending on where you hire your punt.

 Depending on your punting skills allow 1 to 2 hours to make the most of your journey. .... Let's get started

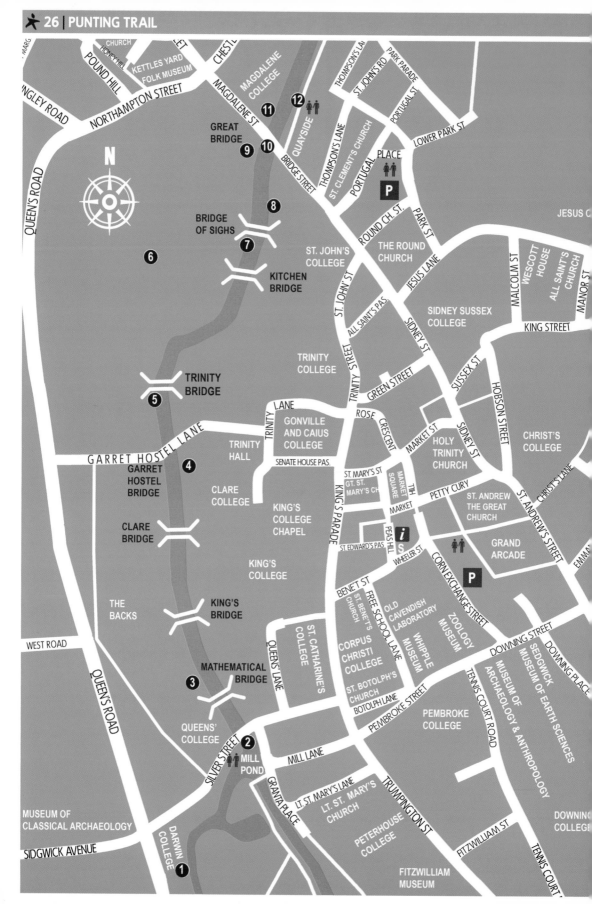

Punting Technique
Top tips to punt like a pro.

About Punting

Punts are flat-bottomed, square-ended wooden boats that are propelled along using a long wooden pole, pushed against the riverbed.

Punting is an ancient form of river transportation which dates back to medieval times. Punts were used by fishermen on the River Thames and more generally, to navigate shallow waterways such as those in The Fens. It was in the 1880s that punting became a recreational activity, a tradition that has remained to this day.

The stretch of river along 'The Backs' is shallow with a gravelly riverbed, making it perfect for punting. The wonderful college views mean that this route is very popular, so if you want to avoid the congestion, punt in the morning or early evening.

Where To Hire A Punt

Self hire punting is available at Mill Lane, Quayside, Granta Pool or Trinity College. Self hire punting is charged by the hour. A credit or debit card will be required for the refundable deposit.

Tips On How To Punt

1. Stand on the platform on the back of the punt with one foot in front of the other as shown in the photograph.

2. Lift the pole vertically out of the water. Position the pole close to the side of punt, then let it slide through your fingers until it touches the riverbed.

3. Grip the pole with both hands and start to push, moving your hands up the pole as the punt moves forward. As you push, you should transfer the weight from your front leg to your rear leg to increase momentum.

4. Once your hands near the top of the pole, give the pole a twist to release it from the riverbed. Let the bottom of the pole float towards the surface and trail behind you.

5. Holding the pole close to your body, use the submerged part like a rudder to steer. Finish the steering manoeuvre before starting your next stroke.

IN OXFORD, PUNTERS STAND INSIDE THE PUNT. THIS IS CONSIDERED A FAUX PAS IN CAMBRIDGE!

... START ALONGSIDE DARWIN COLLEGE SOUTH OF THE MILL POND.

DARWIN COLLEGE | LAUNDRESS GREEN

Darwin College was founded in 1964 by Trinity, St. John's and Gonville and Caius Colleges as the first college in Cambridge exclusively for graduate students. The college was the first within the University to admit both men and women.

DARWIN COLLEGE

Darwin College takes its name from the family of Charles Darwin who previously owned the site.

Charles' second son Sir George Darwin was Professor of Astronomy at the University and bought the Old Granary and surrounding dwellings in 1885. The Darwin family lived here until George's son, Sir Charles Darwin, died in 1962. After his death, the family sold the land to the University for the site of the new college.

As you punt along the small channel between Darwin's grounds and its pretty island, notice the moorings for the college punts. Many of the names relate to Charles Darwin's explorations and discoveries.

1 Which other colleges have made their mark on Darwin's punt moorings?

Darwin College

LAUNDRESS GREEN

Return to the Mill Pool towards Silver Street Bridge. The grassy area on the right beside the river is known as Laundress Green. The Green is named after the university washerwomen who once used the land to wash and dry their laundry. The introduction of electricity to Peterhouse in 1884 (the second location in England to use electricity after the House of Parliament) caused uproar amongst the women, as the smut from the generators dirtied their clean sheets. Today, this area is a popular picnic spot.

2 'Conserve' your energy... Which anniversary is recorded at the bridge?

Laundress Green

... HEAD NORTH AND PASS BENEATH SILVER STREET BRIDGE TO CONTINUE YOUR TRAIL.

...PASS BENEATH THE MATHEMATICAL BRIDGE.

MATHEMATICAL BRIDGE | QUEENS' AND KING'S COLLEGES

You are now officially on 'The Backs'. This part of the river is so called as from this point, only the backs of the colleges are visible.

MATHEMATICAL BRIDGE
QUEENS' LANE
❸
QUEENS'

THE MATHEMATICAL BRIDGE AND QUEENS' COLLEGE

The wooden bridge is the famous Mathematical Bridge belonging to Queens' College. The bridge, dating back to 1749 is the subject of two Cambridge myths. Firstly it is said to have originally been built without bolts, with these only being added when the bridge was taken down by students who were unable to put it back together again. Secondly it is rumoured that the bridge was designed by Sir Isaac Newton. Sadly neither story is true. The bridge was built by James Essex the Younger to a design by William Etheridge. Nevertheless, the bridge is very picturesque and one of the most famous landmarks in the city. The red brick building on the right is the President's Lodge. Dating back to 1460, it is the oldest building on the river.

❸ A place to rest beside the river reveals Vera's profession. What was it?

🏃

Mathematical Bridge

KING'S COLLEGE

King's College Chapel

The next bridge belongs to King's College. The large white building to the right of the chapel is The Gibbs' Building built by James Gibbs in 1724. Gibbs was a prominent architect of his time, responsible for many other iconic buildings including the Radcliffe Camera in Oxford and St. Martin in the Fields Church in London.

King's College Chapel is the most iconic of the city's landmarks and due in part to its famous choir, is known throughout the world. The foundation stone of this spectacular building was laid in 1446 by Henry VI. Eighty years, two monarchs and one civil war later, the chapel was finally completed during the reign of Henry VIII.

...CONTINUE TOWARDS CLARE BRIDGE.

🏃... PASS BENEATH CLARE BRIDGE.

CLARE BRIDGE | CLARE COLLEGE | TRINITY HALL

Clare Bridge is the oldest surviving bridge in the city. One of the fourteen stone balls which decorate the bridge has a segment missing. Legend has it that the bridge's architect left this mark of revenge when the college refused to pay him in full!

🏃 CLARE COLLEGE

Clare is the University's second oldest college and was first founded in 1326 as 'University Hall' and then again in 1338 by Lady Elizabeth de Clare, granddaughter of King Edward I.

Elizabeth's early life was filled with tragedy. She was widowed three times before her 28th birthday and subsequently devoted her life and considerable fortune to charitable works. Elizabeth wore a black mourning band decorated with golden tears in memory of her husbands. These tears are featured on the Clare College crest.

Stone Ball on Clare Bridge

🏃 TRINITY HALL

Jerwood Library at Trinity Hall

Trinity Hall, founded in 1350, is the fifth oldest college within the University. In the 1340s, the Black Death wiped out nearly half the country's population. Having lost 700 of his parish priests, the college founder William Bateman, Bishop of Norwich, founded the college in order to boost numbers of clergymen, clerics and lawyers. The college still has strong reputation for the study of law. All University colleges used to be known as 'Halls', later taking the title 'Colleges'. When Henry VIII founded neighbouring Trinity College in 1546, it became clear that in order to differentiate, Trinity Hall would always be known as a 'Hall'. Trinity Hall's small grounds are very pretty. Author Henry James famously said "If I were called upon to mention the prettiest corner of the world, I should draw a thoughtful sigh and point the way to the gardens of Trinity Hall".

4 Look out for Trinity Hall's crest and then use your artistic talents to sketch its features.

🏃... PASS BENEATH GARRET HOSTEL BRIDGE.

... CONTINUE TOWARDS TRINITY COLLEGE BRIDGE.

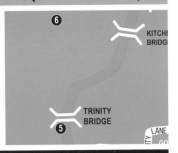

RINITY COLLEGE | WREN LIBRARY | ST JOHN'S NEW COURT

rinity College is the largest and wealthiest of all the colleges. Alumni include n incredible 32 Nobel prize winners (University members hold 82 in total) and mong many others include Sir Isaac Newton, Lord Byron, Sir Francis Bacon nd HRH Prince Charles.

TRINITY COLLEGE AND THE WREN LIBRARY

5 Check mate! Which chess piece is among the decorative features on Trinity Bridge?

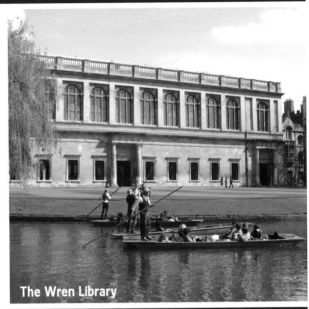

ss beneath Trinity College Bridge. Trinity's ren Library is now on your right. Designed by Sir ristopher Wren, the library was completed in 584. It is one of the first libraries to have been built th the reader in mind - note the numerous large ndows, designed to let in as much natural light as ssible. The library is full of historically important oks including early editions of Shakespeare's works, ces from Sir Isaac Newton's own collection and the iginal manuscript of AA Milne's 'Winnie The Pooh'. A and his son Christopher Robin studied at Trinity.

The Wren Library

ST. JOHN'S COLLEGE AND THE WEDDING CAKE

St. John's New Court

Follow the river as it bears to the right. Ahead of you on the left is the majestic New Court of St. John's College. The Gothic style structure was completed in 1831 and was the first college building to be built on the west side of the river. The building is affectionately known as 'The Wedding Cake'. During May Week (which confusingly takes place in June after the end of exams), the lawn to the front of the New Court is the stunning location for St. John's May Ball fireworks. Many of the colleges have May Balls and these are famously lavish affairs, often showcasing the leading bands and artists of the time. St. John's Ball was named the seventh best party in the world by Time Magazine.

6 One architectural feature of the 'Wedding Cake' can be described as timeless in more ways than one. Why?

... CONTINUE PUNTING TO KITCHEN BRIDGE (ST. JOHN'S OLD BRIDGE).

🏃... CONTINUE TO KITCHEN BRIDGE.

KITCHEN BRIDGE | THE BRIDGE OF SIGHS

St. John's is the only college to have two bridges. The first is the Old Bridge, also known as Kitchen Bridge and the second, the famous Bridge of Sighs.

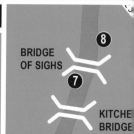

BRIDGE OF SIGHS

KITCHEN BRIDGE

🏃 ST. JOHN'S COLLEGE - KITCHEN BRIDGE

7 Kitchen Bridge bears the marks of nature's force. What happened and when?

Pass beneath Kitchen Bridge. St. John's Lady Margaret Boat Club is the oldest on the river. The annual University Boat Race began when members of the club challenged Oxford to a race in 1829. Oxford (or 'The Other Place' as it is known here) won. Since 1856, the University Boat Race has been held every year, apart from during the two World Wars. Overall, the two Universities are very closely matched, but Cambridge currently has a small lead. Oarsmen of the LMBC wear bright scarlet jackets and these were the origin for the word 'blazer', now used to describe sports jackets in general.

Kitchen Bridge

🏃 ST. JOHN'S COLLEGE - THE BRIDGE OF SIGHS

The Bridge of Sighs

Pass beneath the Bridge of Sighs. This beautiful bridge was built in 1831 to link the New Court to the main part of the college. The bridge is one of the most famous sights within the city. Although its only similarity is that it is a covered bridge, it is named after its predecessor in Venice. Others say the structure takes its name from the sound students make when crossing the bridge after leaving exams! On two separate occasions, in 1963 and 1968, student pranksters suspended a car beneath the bridge. Both times, the vehicle was punted along the river before being hoisted up by ropes.

8 It's all Greek (and Latin) to me! What is requested of passing punters here?

🏃... CONTINUE ON TOWARDS THE GREAT BRIDGE.

🏃 **... CONTINUE PAST ST. JOHN'S COLLEGE TOWARDS THE GREAT BRIDGE.**

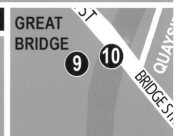

GREAT
BRIDGE
⑨ ⑩

ST. JOHN'S COLLEGE OLD AND NEW | THE GREAT BRIDGE

Do the swans seem to glide a little more quickly when they pass St. John's? Perhaps this is because according to an ancient law, apart from the monarchy, fellows of St. John's are the only people permitted to eat swan. Swan traps were originally built into the college walls along the river.

🏃 THE OLD AND THE NEW

The grass to your left was once the site of the 1921 St. John's College bathhouse. When the bathhouse was proposed, one of the fellows of the college is reported to have replied "What do they need baths for? They are only here for eight weeks at a time!". After 1945, the number of students attending St. John's increased dramatically, leaving accommodation bursting at the seams. The large modern building to your left is a 1960s student accommodation block built to meet this demand. The building was funded by the Cripps Foundation and is known simply as 'Cripps'. Tucked away behind Cripps is The School of Pythagoras. Dating back to around 1200AD, this is St. John's oldest building and is still in use as a theatre for the college drama society. The small channel flowing into the college grounds belongs to St. John's and leads to a private punt mooring. The grounds beyond belong to Magdalene College.

⑨ Use this 'benchmark' to discover how Magdalene remembers Derek Oulton.

Looking back at the Bridge of Sighs

🏃 THE GREAT BRIDGE

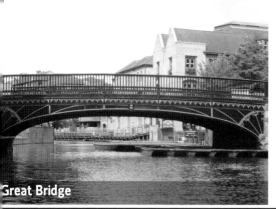

Great Bridge

The Great Bridge, sometimes also referred to as Magdalene Bridge, stands at the site of the very first river crossing in the city. The original bridge was a wooden construction and is mentioned in records dating back to the middle 800s. In fact, this bridge gave the city its name - Bridge over the River Cam - Cambridge.

⑩ How long did Arthur's bridge last before it needed reconstructing?

🏃 **... PASS BENEATH THE GREAT BRIDGE.**

... YOU ARE NOW IN THE QUAYSIDE AREA OF CAMBRIDGE.

MAGDALENE COLLEGE | QUAYSIDE | JESUS GREEN

Cambridge was once an important trading town which relied heavily on the river as a means of transporting goods to and from the area. Quayside was the town's port.

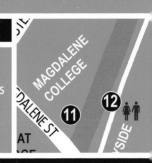

MAGDALENE COLLEGE

Magdalene College (pronounced 'Maudlin') stands beside the river. Magdalene began life in 1428 as a hostel for Benedictine monks. In 1542, under the guidance of Sir Thomas Audley, Lord Chancellor to Henry VIII, the College of St. Mary Magdalene was founded on the site. Magdalene is home to the Pepys Library bequeathed by the 17th Century diarist and famous graduate of the college, Samuel Pepys.

Magdalene College

11 Which stone creature has a bird's eye view from Magdalene College?

JESUS GREEN

Jesus Lock

12 Whose stony face spouts water into The Cam at Quayside?

Most people use this point on the river to turn around and punt back to their starting point. If you want to extend your trip, carry on a short distance towards Jesus Lock. This is the farthest point that is accessible to punts and you will pass several narrow boats. Motorised boat trips depart from the opposit side of the lock. To the right of this area is Jesus Green, one of Cambridge's many open green spaces. The Green is the location of the annual real ale festival and a summer comedy week. It is also home to one of the UK's longest outdoor swimming pools. It measures 100 yards long which is around 90m!

With your punting skills now finely honed it's time to head back to your starting point.

Family Trail
A special set of clues for big and little kids to enjoy solving together.

Springtime at Gonville and Caius College

This trail follows the same route as the City Highlights. For a bigger challenge you can try to solve both sets of clues in parallel. You can also refer to the detailed sightseeing guide in the City Highlights pages as you complete the Family Trail.

Full Trail   2.5 to 3 hours,
Shorter Trail   2 to 2.5 hours.   .... Let's get started

KEY

- **S** Start point
- **F** Finish Point
- **1** Clue number and location
- Route
- Public Toilets
- **P** Car park
- **i** Visitor Information Centre

MIDSUMMER COMMON →

RIVER CAM

CHESTERTON ROAD

CASTLE MOUND

JESUS GREEN

JESUS COLLEGE

JESUS LANE

CASTLE ROW
CASTLE STREET
ST PETER'S ST
ST PETER'S CHURCH
HONEY HILL
POUND HILL
NORTHAMPTON STREET
KETTLES YARD FOLK MUSEUM
MARGARET RD
HAYMARKET RD
ALBION ROW
PLEASANT
LANGLEY ROAD
QUEEN'S ROAD

AVENUE
FORD STREET

CHESTERTON LANE
MAGDALENE ST
MAGDALENE COLLEGE
BRIDGE STREET
QUAYSIDE
THOMPSON'S LANE
ST JOHN'S RD
PARK PARADE
PORTUGAL ST
LOWER PARK ST
PARK ST

GREAT BRIDGE

BRIDGE OF SIGHS
KITCHEN BRIDGE
ST JOHN'S COLLEGE
ST JOHN'S STREET
ALL SAINT'S PAS.
ST CLEMENT'S CHURCH
PORTUGAL PLACE
ROUND CH. ST.
THE ROUND CHURCH
JESUS LANE
SIDNEY SUSSEX COLLEGE
MALCOLM ST
WESCOTT HOUSE
ALL SAINT'S CHURCH
MANOR ST
KING STREET

TRINITY BRIDGE
TRINITY COLLEGE
TRINITY STREET
GREEN STREET
SIDNEY ST
SUSSEX ST
HOBSON STREET
CHRIST'S PIECES
CHRIST'S COLLEGE
CHRIST'S LANE

GARRET HOSTEL LANE
TRINITY LANE
GONVILLE AND CAIUS COLLEGE
TRINITY HALL
SENATE HOUSE PAS.
ROSE CRESCENT
MARKET ST
HOLY TRINITY CHURCH
ST ANDREW'S STREET
BUS STATION
DRUMMER ST

GARRET HOSTEL BRIDGE
CLARE BRIDGE
CLARE COLLEGE
KING'S COLLEGE CHAPEL
ST MARY'S ST
GT. ST. MARY'S CH.
KING'S PARADE
MARKET SQUARE
MARKET
PETTY CURY
ST ANDREW THE GREAT CHURCH
GRAND ARCADE
EMMANUEL STREET
EMMANUEL COLLEGE

THE BACKS
KING'S COLLEGE
KING'S BRIDGE
ST EDWARD'S PAS.
PEAS HILL
WHEELER ST
CORN EXCHANGE STREET
P
DOWNING STREET
DOWNING PLACE
PARK TERR.

WEST ROAD
QUEEN'S ROAD
QUEENS' LANE
MATHEMATICAL BRIDGE
ST CATHARINE'S COLLEGE
BENET ST
ST BENET'S CHURCH
CORPUS CHRISTI COLLEGE
FREE SCHOOL LANE
OLD CAVENDISH LABORATORY
WHIPPLE MUSEUM
ZOOLOGY MUSEUM
TENNIS COURT ROAD
MUSEUM OF ARCHAEOLOGY & ANTHROPOLOGY
SEDGWICK MUSEUM OF EARTH SCIENCES
REGENT STREET

QUEENS' COLLEGE
SILVER STREET
MILL POND
MILL LANE
ST. BOTOLPH'S CHURCH
BOTOLPH LANE
PEMBROKE STREET
PEMBROKE COLLEGE
DOWNING COLLEGE
TENNIS COURT

MUSEUM OF CLASSICAL ARCHAEOLOGY
SIDGWICK AVENUE
DARWIN COLLEGE
GRANTA PLACE
LT. ST. MARY'S LANE
ST. MARY'S CHURCH
PETERHOUSE COLLEGE
TRUMPINGTON ST
FITZWILLIAM ST
FITZWILLIAM MUSEUM

N

★ BENE'T STREET

Begin at St. Bene't's Church on Bene't Street

1 Look within the churchyard to find something which would have kept local people refreshed years ago. What is it?

★ FREE SCHOOL LANE

Enter Free School Lane next to the church and continue to the end where the lane meets Pembroke Street.

2 Look up to find the names of four famous men. What is Newton's symbol?

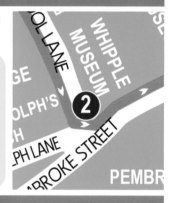

★ FITZWILLIAM MUSEUM

Follow the trail along Tennis Court Road, turn right into Fitzwilliam St. and continue to the Fitzwilliam Museum.

3 The photo on the left is of a figure above the main entrance to the Fitzwilliam Museum. What musical instrument is he holding?

★ LITTLE ST. MARY'S LANE

Follow the trail back towards the city centre and turn left into Little St. Mary's Lane.

4 Who guards the door of Number 7?

★ THE CITY HIGHLIGHTS PAGES CONTAIN A DETAILED SIGHTSEEING GUIDE FOR THIS ROUTE.

THE BACKS

Walk along Granta Place, through Laundress Lane and turn left along Silver Street to 'The Backs'.

5 Find the Rotary Map at the beginning of the pathway along The Backs. How many chapels are within 250m of the corner of Queens' Lane and Silver Street?

GARRET HOSTEL LANE

Continue along the path on The Backs and turn right along Garret Hostel Lane. Continue to the bridge.

6 Rearrange the letters SEARCH to make a new word. Look at Clare Bridge (decorated with stone balls). How many ****** does Clare Bridge have?

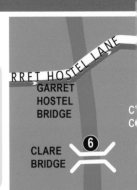

SENATE HOUSE PASSAGE AND TRINITY STREET

Turn right at the end of Garret Hostel Lane and then left into Senate House Passage. Walk to the end and turn left on Trinity Street. Your clue is located on the left, on the walls of Gonville and Caius College.

7 These men look down on us with stony faces. Who can be found between the 'JERS'?

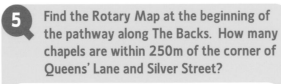

GREEN STREET AND SIDNEY SUSSEX COLLEGE

Turn right into Green Street and walk to the end of the street to face Sidney Sussex College.

8 There are several stone shields on the walls beneath the bell tower but how many are decorated?

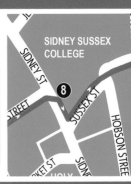

FROM HERE YOU CAN TAKE A SHORTCUT. SEE THE TOP OF THE NEXT PAGE.

FOR THE SHORTER TRAIL, SKIP TO CLUE 13. FOR THE LONGER TRAIL, READ ON.

Turn right along Sidney Sussex Street then left into Sussex Street. Bear left into King Street.

 9 Find the pub on King Street which has the word Champion in its name. What sport does it link to?

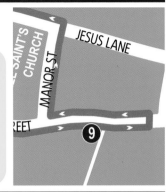

JESUS LANE

From King Street, walk to the end of Manor Street and turn left along Jesus Lane.

10 Which pair of creatures guards the entrance to Westcott House on Jesus Lane?

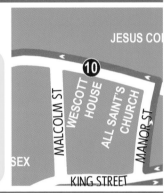

PORTUGAL PLACE

From Jesus Lane, turn right along Park Street to Portugal Place (next to the Maypole Pub).

11 Scientist Francis Crick once lived at no. 19 Portugal Place. What hangs outside his house?

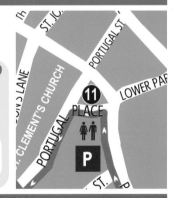

CASTLE HILL

Turn right along Bridge Street and continue to the crossroads with Magdalene Street and Chesterton Lane. The site of the former Cambridge castle is a little way up the hill if you want to take a look.

12 What did the Folk Museum used to be?

BOTH TRAILS CONTINUE ON THE NEXT PAGE.

⭐ MAGDALENE STREET AND THE GREAT BRIDGE.

Go to Magdalene Street near the Great Bridge.

13 The Pickerel Pub is the oldest pub in Cambridge, but what is a pickerel? The pub's sign may help you.

⭐ BRIDGE STREET AND THE ROUND CHURCH.

Walk along Bridge Street to the Round Church.

14 How many stained glass windows decorate the ROUND walls of the Round Church?

⭐ SAINT JOHN'S STREET AND ST. JOHN'S COLLEGE.

Turn right into Saint John's Street. Continue to the main gate of St John's College.

15 Which bird sits at the feet of St. John above the main entrance to the college?

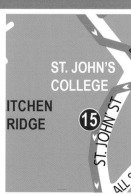

⭐ TRINITY STREET AND TRINITY COLLEGE.

Continue along Trinity Street to Trinity College.

16 Look closely at the statue of Henry VIII above the Great Gate. What is he holding in his right hand?

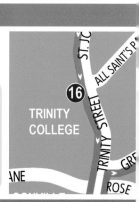

⭐ JUST FOUR CLUES TO GO...

★ GREAT ST. MARY'S CHURCH

Continue along Trinity Street to Great St. Mary's Church.

 17 Near the church, which member of the family offers a cup of tea?

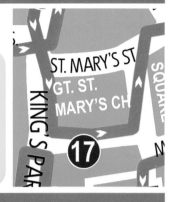

★ THE MARKET SQUARE AND GUILDHALL

Go to The Guildhall on the Market Square.

18 Which two creatures have 'time on their hands'?

★ PEAS HILL AND ST. EDWARD'S PASSAGE.

Walk along Peas Hill and turn right into St. Edward's Passage.

19 St. Edward's Church is linked to two colleges. Make a note of them and sketch their college shields.

★ KING'S PARADE.

Turn left at the end of St. Edward's Passage onto King's Parade.

 20 You can toast your success here if you can find out what George Cunningham's job was.

★ CONGRATULATIONS, YOU'VE FINISHED! FOR HOW TO PLAY THE QUIZ GO TO PAGE 64.

Live The City Bitesize

The bitesize section of this guide contains more information about the city and its University. A summary of all the colleges is included with a look at the most iconic building in the city, King's College Chapel. Read about the amazing range of museums you can visit. Finally, discover some surprising stories and our Top 10 guide of things to do in the city.

LIVE THE CITY BITESIZE CONTENTS

SIR RICHARD ATTENBOROUGH WAS BORN IN CAMBRIDGE IN 1923.

Cambridge
The essential history

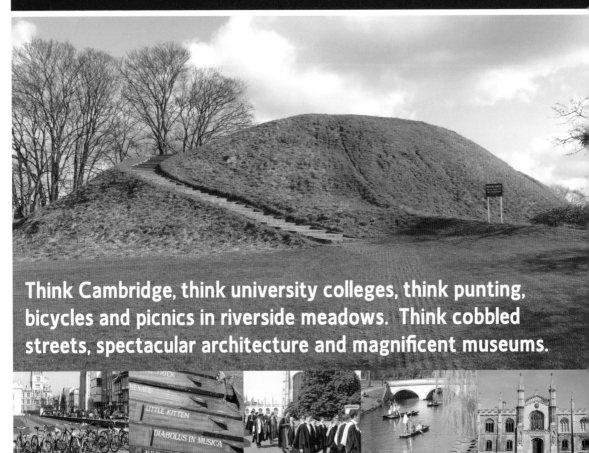

Think Cambridge, think university colleges, think punting, bicycles and picnics in riverside meadows. Think cobbled streets, spectacular architecture and magnificent museums.

The Origins of Cambridge: A Timeline

The earliest known settlers in the area were the Romans who arrived in around 40 AD. They were attracted by the small hill (now known as Castle Hill), which provided an excellent lookout across the flat Fen countryside and the small river.

Some 400 years later, when the Romans left the area, the town fell into decline and remained virtually deserted for several centuries.

During the 9th and 10th Centuries, the area was once again occupied, first by the Danes and then the Saxons, both of whom reestablished Cambridge as a trading town. At this time, the town was known by the Anglo Saxon name of Grantebrycge with the River Cam known as the River Granta. In 1068, just two years after King Harold's fateful encounter with an arrow, the Normans arrived in Cambridge. Under their strict rule, the town became one of the most important centres of commerce in the country.

he town continued to prosper with trade. In 1207, ing John granted a charter to Cambridge, giving ew rights to the town (a copy of the charter is on isplay in The Guildhall). Religion also began to play n increasingly important part in the town during the 3th Century, with the arrival of Dominican, Carmelite nd Franciscan friars who each preached their beliefs o the local people.

wo years later, the town experienced a momentous urning point. In 1209, rioting between the students nd townsfolk of Oxford became so violent and oody that a group of scholars and their tutors fled ne city and came to Cambridge. This year is ommemorated as the official birth of the University.

ttle is known of the early days of the University, nce most of the documents from this time were estroyed in a violent uprising between scholars and ownsfolk in 1261. The people of Cambridge were uickly coming to realise that the University was stablishing a powerful hold over the town. This was 1ade abundantly clear when King Henry III's court ave a royal pardon to all 28 scholars involved in the prising, yet sentenced the 16 townsfolk to death.

Peterhouse

ne first college, Peterhouse, was founded in 1284. om this point, Cambridge's development was ominated by the growth of the University. By the id 15th Century, large areas of land were being aimed to expand the University, often resulting in ne demolition of nearby houses and businesses.

ne 16th Century saw a rapid expansion within the niversity, with no less than six new colleges founded uring the 100-year period. In 1538, Henry VIII osed all the Cambridge friaries, handing over their nd to the University.

The town's population also increased steadily during the 16th and 17th Centuries despite a severe outbreak of plague in 1630. As the University grew, so the town flourished. In 1766 the now world famous Addenbrookes Hospital was founded and in 1780 the first bank was opened in the town.

Cambridge Train Station

In 1845, the arrival of the railway brought a dramatic change to the town, quickly wiping out river-borne trade and the port. The new railway did however provide a valuable link to London bringing new opportunities and prosperity to the town. Political reforms saw the establishment of a properly elected town council and many of the ancient university privileges, which had caused such tension, were revoked.

Despite its prominent position throughout the centuries, it was only in 1951, that Cambridge was awarded city status. Throughout the 1960s and 70s, the city expanded rapidly, particularly north of the river, with new housing estates to accommodate the growing population.

In 1992, the city's second university, Anglia Polytechnic (now Anglia Ruskin University), was opened. No longer just a university city, Cambridge today is a centre of excellence in technological and scientific research and is often referred to as 'Silicon Fen'.

William Gates Building
Computer Laboratory

It is a city that proudly displays its great past and strives towards an even greater future.

Cambridge University AD 1209...

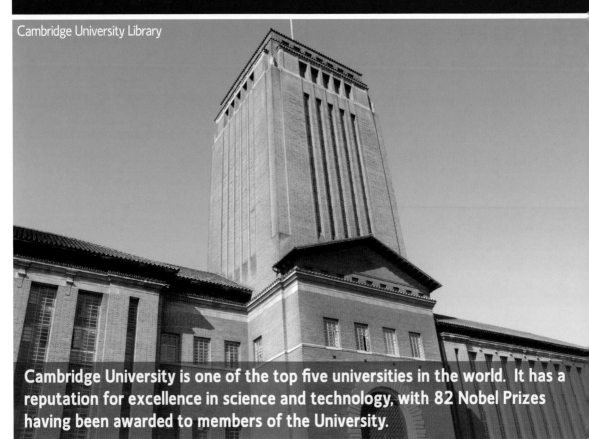

Cambridge University Library

Cambridge University is one of the top five universities in the world. It has a reputation for excellence in science and technology, with 82 Nobel Prizes having been awarded to members of the University.

In 1209, rioting between the students and townsfolk of Oxford became so violent that a group of scholars and their tutors fled and came to Cambridge. This year is commemorated as the official birth of the university.

Today, the University consists of 31 colleges and more than 150 departments. Each college is run independently and is responsible for recruiting its own teaching staff and selecting its undergraduates.

Teaching staff and academics from the different colleges make up the various departments (ie. Chemistry, Engineering, Physics) and lectures are then conducted within these departments.

College 'fellows' are academics affiliated to the University who conduct research, lectures and student supervision across a broad range of subjects. Each college has its own unique character and is special within its own right. With the exception of the examination period, it is normally possible to visit the colleges and this is highly recommended.

To help you select the ones you would like to visit, we have compiled a list of all the Cambridge college including location and contact details. The list is in chronological order of the date each college was founded.

All The Colleges
in chronological order

1. PETERHOUSE — FOUNDED IN 1284

INFO: The oldest college within the University and also the smallest. It was founded by Hugo de Balsham, Bishop of Ely.

SIZE: 250 undergraduates and 90 graduate students.

ALUMNI: Notable 'Petreans' include Thomas Gray (17th Century Poet), Charles Babbage (inventor of the forerunner to the modern computer), Michael Portillo (politician and broadcaster) and Sam Mendes (film director).

ADDRESS: Trumpington Road, CB2 1RD. Telephone: 01223 338200

VISITING: Free to visit.
Check with the Porters' Lodge for opening times.

2. CLARE COLLEGE — FOUNDED IN 1326

Founded in 1326 as University Hall, re-founded in 1338 as Clare Hall and known as Clare College from 1856.

INFO: Dr. Edward Atkinson was Master at Clare for an impressive 59 years between 1856 and 1915 - a University record.

SIZE: 460 undergraduates and 180 graduate students.

ALUMNI: Hugh Latimer (Protestant Reformer), Dr. Rowan Williams (Archbishop of Canterbury) and Sir David Attenborough (broadcaster and naturalist).

ADDRESS: Trinity Lane, CB2 1TL. Telephone: 01223 333200

VISITING: £2.50 admission charge (includes entry to The Great Hall and Chapel).
Check with the Porters' Lodge for opening times.

3. PEMBROKE COLLEGE — FOUNDED IN 1347

INFO: Sir Christopher Wren made his architectural debut at Pembroke, with the design of the college chapel. The pretty grounds contain a statue to Pembroke graduate, William Pitt The Younger.

SIZE: 420 undergraduates and 400 graduate students.

ALUMNI: William Pitt The Younger (Youngest British Prime Minister), Peter Cook (comedian) and Ted Hughes (poet).

ADDRESS: Trumpington Street, CB2 1RF. Telephone: 01223 338100

VISITING: Free to visit.
Check with the Porters' Lodge for opening times.

WILLIAM WOOTON BECAME THE UNIVERSITY'S YOUNGEST EVER STUDENT IN 1675 AGED JUST 9.

🏃 4. GONVILLE AND CAIUS — FOUNDED IN 1347

INFO: The three sided courts were designed by the college's second founder, Dr. John Caius to allow air to circulate freely within the grounds to promote good health.

SIZE: 420 undergraduates and 400 graduate students.

ALUMNI: Stephen Hawking (mathematician and author), Francis Crick (Nobel prize winning scientist) and Sir David Frost (broadcaster).

ADDRESS: Trinity Street, Cambridge. Telephone: 01223 332400

VISITING: Free to visit.
Check with the Porters' Lodge for opening times.

🏃 5. TRINITY HALL — FOUNDED IN 1350

INFO: The college gardens were described by author Henry James as "The prettiest corner in the world". Take a moment to see for yourself whether you agree with him.

SIZE: 359 undergraduates and 253 graduate students.

ALUMNI: Donald McLean (Soviet Spy and one of 'The Cambridge Five'), Hans Blix (former UN Chief Weapons Inspector) and Rachel Weisz (Oscar winning actress).

ADDRESS: Trinity Lane, CB2 1TJ. Telephone: 01223 332500

VISITING: Free to visit.
Check with the Porters' Lodge for opening times.

🏃 6. CORPUS CHRISTI COLLEGE — FOUNDED IN 1352

INFO: Corpus Christi is the only college within Oxbridge to have been founded by the citizens of the town rather than wealthy aristocracy. The incredible Corpus 'Chronophage' clock is the city's newest landmark attraction.

SIZE: 250 undergraduates and 150 graduate students.

ALUMNI: Christopher Marlowe (poet and dramatist) and Christopher Isherwood (novelist).

ADDRESS: Trumpington St, CB2 1RH. Telephone: 01223 338000

VISITING: Free to visit.
Check with the Porters' Lodge for opening times.

🏃 7. MAGDALENE COLLEGE — FOUNDED IN 1428

INFO: Magdalene's Benson Court was designed by Edwin Lutyens, best known for having planned the city of New Delhi in India. The college is home to the Pepys Library.

SIZE: 348 undergraduates and 246 graduate students.

ALUMNI: Samuel Pepys (diarist), CS Lewis (author), George Mallory (mountaineer).

ADDRESS: Magdalene Street, CB3 0AG. Telephone: 01223 332100

VISITING: Free to visit (including Pepys Library when open).
Check with the Porters' Lodge for opening times.

🏃 **SEE UNIVERSITY SPORTING FIXTURES LISTS IN RYDERS AND AMIES ON KING'S PARADE.**

8. KING'S COLLEGE — FOUNDED IN 1441

INFO: Originally intended exclusively for boys educated at Eton, the college now has one of the highest intakes from state schools. Home to the world famous King's College Chapel.

SIZE: 392 undergraduates and 280 graduate students.

ALUMNI: John Maynard Keynes (Economist), Salman Rushdie (author) and Rupert Brooke (First World War poet).

ADDRESS: King's Parade, CB2 1ST. Telephone: 01223 331100

VISITING: £5 admission charge (Chapel and grounds). Entrance to the college grounds is via the chapel on Trinity Lane. Chapel opening times vary according to term dates.

9. QUEENS' COLLEGE — FOUNDED IN 1446

INFO: Unlike other colleges within the University, the head of Queens' holds the title President rather than Master. Home to the famous Mathematical Bridge.

SIZE: 490 undergraduates and 270 graduate students.

ALUMNI: Graham Swift (author) and Stephen Fry (comedian, author and presenter).

ADDRESS: Silver Street, CB3 9ET. Telephone: 01223 335511

VISITING: £2.50 (includes the Old Hall and Chapel). Entrance via the Visitors' Gate in Queens' Lane. Check with the Porters' Lodge for opening times.

10. ST. CATHARINE'S COLLEGE — FOUNDED IN 1473

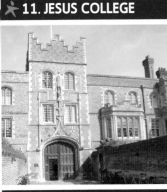

INFO: Named after Catharine of Alexandria, the patron saint of scholars, the college is decorated with her symbol, the Catharine Wheel.

SIZE: 410 undergraduates and 150 graduate students.

ALUMNI: John Addenbrooke (founder of Addenbrooke's hospital), Jeremy Paxman (TV presenter and journalist) and Sir Ian McKellan (actor).

ADDRESS: Trumpington Street, CB2 1RL. Telephone: 01223 338300

VISITING: Free to visit. Check with the Porters' Lodge for opening times.

11. JESUS COLLEGE — FOUNDED IN 1496

INFO: Full name: "The College of the Blessed Virgin Mary, Saint John the Evangelist and the glorious Virgin Saint Radegund near Cambridge".

SIZE: 489 undergraduates and 270 graduate students.

ALUMNI: Thomas Cranmer (martyred Archbishop of Canterbury), Alistair Cooke (broadcaster), Prince Edward, Earl of Wessex.

ADDRESS: Jesus Lane, CB5 8BL. Telephone: 01223 339339

VISITING: Free to visit. Check with the Porters' Lodge for opening times.

THE QUEEN MOTHER WAS THE FIRST WOMAN AWARDED A DEGREE IN THE SENATE HOUSE IN 1948.

 12. CHRIST'S COLLEGE FOUNDED IN 1505

INFO:	Founded by St. John's founder Lady Margaret Beaufort.
SIZE:	420 undergraduates and 110 graduate students.
ALUMNI:	John Milton (poet), Charles Darwin (naturalist and author) and Sacha Baron Cohen (satirist and comedic actor).
ADDRESS:	St Andrew's St, CB2 3BU. Telephone: 01223 334900
VISITING:	Free to visit. Check with the Porters' Lodge for opening times.

13. ST. JOHN'S COLLEGE FOUNDED IN 1511

INFO:	St. John's' Boat Club initiated the first University Boat Race.
SIZE:	534 undergraduates and 340 graduate students.
ALUMNI:	William Wordsworth (poet), William Wilberforce (politician and abolishionist) and Sir Maurice Wilkes (founding father of modern computer science).
ADDRESS:	Saint John's Street, CB2 1TP. Telephone: 01223 338600
VISITING:	£3 (£2 for children and students) Check with the Porters' Lodge for opening times.

14. TRINITY COLLEGE FOUNDED IN 1546

INFO:	The wealthiest of all the University colleges.
SIZE:	663 undergraduates and 430 graduate students.
ALUMNI:	Sir Isaac Newton (physicist, mathematician and astronomer), Lord Byron (poet) and Ernest Rutherford ('father of nuclear physics').
ADDRESS:	Trinity St, CB2 1TQ. Telephone: 01223 338400
VISITING:	£3 (£1.50 for children and students). Check with the Porters' Lodge for opening times.

15. EMMANUEL COLLEGE FOUNDED IN 1584

INFO:	The college grounds include an outdoor swimming pool which has been in use since at least 1744.
SIZE:	465 undergraduates and 185 graduate students.
ALUMNI:	John Harvard (founder of Harvard University), Graham Chapman (comedian) and Sebastian Faulks (author). St Andrew's St, CB2 3AP. Telephone: 01223 334200
ADDRESS:	Free to visit.
VISITING:	Check with the Porters' Lodge for opening times.

 16. SIDNEY SUSSEX COLLEGE FOUNDED IN 1596

INFO:	Former student Oliver Cromwell's head is buried in a secret location near Sidney's chapel.
SIZE:	350 undergraduates and 100 graduate students.
ALUMNI:	Oliver Cromwell (he didn't actually graduate), David Owen (British politician) and Carol Vorderman (TV presenter).
ADDRESS:	Sidney Street, CB2 3HU. Telephone: 01223 338800
VISITING:	Free to visit. Check with the Porters' Lodge for opening times.

THE FIRST EDITION OF THE CAMBRIDGE STUDENT PAPER VARSITY WAS PUBLISHED IN 1931.

17. DOWNING COLLEGE   FOUNDED IN 1800

INFO: Downing has no courts. Its buildings are neo-Grecian in design.
SIZE: 403 undergraduates and 252 graduate students.
ALUMNI: Michael Atherton (England cricketer), John Cleese (comedian and actor) and Thandie Newton (actress).
Regent Street, CB2 1DQ. Telephone: 01223 334800
ADDRESS: Free to visit.
VISITING: Check with the Porters' Lodge for opening times.

18. FITZWILLIAM COLLEGE   FOUNDED IN 1869

INFO: Originally a non-collegiate body, Fitzwilliam was granted full college status in 1966.
SIZE: 474 undergraduates and 180 graduate students.
ALUMNI: Norman Lamont (Former Chancellor of the Exchequer), Vince Cable (MP) and Nick Drake (singer/songwriter).
ADDRESS: Storey's Way, CB3 0DG. Telephone: 01223 332000
VISITING: Free to visit.
Check with the Porters' Lodge for opening times.

19. GIRTON COLLEGE   FOUNDED IN 1869

INFO: Now co-educational, the once all female college was built outside the city centre to discourage male visitors.
SIZE: 503 undergraduates and 201 graduate students.
ALUMNI: Sandi Toksvig (comedian and presenter), Anna Maxted (novelist) and Julie Kirkbride (British politician).
ADDRESS: Huntingdon Road, CB3 0JG. Telephone: 01223 338999
VISITING: Free to visit.
Check with the Porters' Lodge for opening times.

20. NEWNHAM COLLEGE   FOUNDED IN 1875

INFO: The second all female college to be founded, Newnham is still a women only establishment.
SIZE: 400 undergraduates and 150 graduate students.
ALUMNI: Diane Abbott (MP), Rosalind Franklin (chemist who worked alongside Watson and Crick) and Sylvia Plath (poet).
Sidgwick Avenue, CB3 9DF. Telephone: 01223 335700
ADDRESS: Free to visit.
VISITING: Check with the Porters' Lodge for opening times.

21. SELWYN COLLEGE   FOUNDED IN 1882

INFO: Founded by George Augustus Selwyn, First Bishop of New Zealand.
SIZE: 360 undergraduates and 130 graduate students.
ALUMNI: Hugh Laurie (comedian and actor), John Sentamu (Archbishop of York) and Clive Anderson (comedian and presenter).
ADDRESS: Grange Road, CB3 9DQ. Telephone: 01223 335846
VISITING: Free to visit.
Check with the Porters' Lodge for opening times.

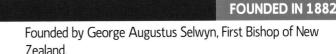

TRINITY COLLEGE CLAIMS TO HAVE INVENTED AN ENGLISH VERSION OF CRÈME BRÛLÉE.

22. HUGHES HALL

FOUNDED IN 1885

INFO:	Hughes Hall began as a teacher training college and was an early promoter of women's education.
SIZE:	60 undergraduates and 325 graduate students.
ALUMNI:	Hilary Finch (writer for The Times), Alison Uttley (children's author) and Lavinia Byrne (writer and broadcaster).
ADDRESS:	Mortimer Rd, CB1 2EW. Telephone: 01223 334898.
VISITING:	Not open to visitors.

23. ST EDMUND'S COLLEGE

FOUNDED IN 1896

INFO:	The most international college within the University, with students from over 70 different countries.
SIZE:	100 undergraduates and 230 graduate students.
ALUMNI:	Georges Lemaitre (cosmologist and developer of the Big Bang Theory).
ADDRESS:	Mount Pleasant, CB3 0BN. Tel: 01223 336250.
VISITING:	Normally closed to visitors. Visits may be possible by prior arrangement. Contact the Porter's Lodge for details.

24. MURRAY EDWARDS COLLEGE (FORMERLY NEW HALL)

FOUNDED IN 1954

INFO:	Renamed in 2008 after the first president, Rosemary Murray and benefactors Ros and Steve Edwards.
SIZE:	360 undergraduates, 70 graduates.
ALUMNI:	Sue Perkins (comedian), Tilda Swinton (actress) and Misha Husain (BBC news presenter)
ADDRESS:	Huntingdon Road, CB3 0DF. Telephone: 01223 762100.
VISITING:	Free to visit. Check with the Porters' Lodge for opening times.

25. CHURCHILL COLLEGE

FOUNDED IN 1960

INFO:	Inspired by Churchill's visit to the Massachusetts Institute of Technology. Specialises in science and engineering.
SIZE:	450 undergraduates, 280 graduate students.
ALUMNI:	Michael Burrows (inventor of the Altavista internet search engine), Sir Christopher Frayling (writer).
ADDRESS:	Storey's Way, CB3 0DS. Telephone: 01223 336000.
VISITING:	Free to visit. Check with the Porters' Lodge for opening times.

26. DARWIN COLLEGE

FOUNDED IN 1964

INFO:	The largest postgraduate college within the University. It was founded by Trinity, Gonville and Caius and St. John's.
SIZE:	591 graduates
ALUMNI:	Dian Fossey (American Zoologist), Paul Clement (former Solicitor General of United States)
ADDRESS:	Silver Street, CB3 9EU. Telephone: 01223 335660.
VISITING:	Normally closed to visitors. Visits may be possible by prior arrangement. Contact the Porter's Lodge for details.

THE UNIVERSITY OF CAMBRIDGE HAS AROUND 17,500 FULL TIME STUDENTS.

27. LUCY CAVENDISH COLLEGE — FOUNDED IN 1965

INFO:	A college for women over 21 only.
SIZE:	110 undergraduates and 110 graduate students.
ALUMNI:	Noeleen Heyzer (Director of United Nations Development fund for Women), Kelly Smith (Author), Gill Saxon (Writer).
ADDRESS:	Lady Margaret Road, CB3 0BU. Tel: 01223 332190
VISITING:	Normally closed to visitors. Visits may be possible by prior arrangement. Contact the Porter's Lodge for details.

28. WOLFSON COLLEGE — FOUNDED IN 1965

INFO:	Originally named University College, Wolfson was renamed in 1972 after a generous donation from the Wolfson Foundation.
SIZE:	110 undergraduates and 650 graduate students.
ALUMNI:	Matthew Fisher (musician of Procol Harem fame), Sabiha Sumar (Pakistani filmmaker) and Ken Yeang (acclaimed architect). Barton Road, CB3 9BB. Telephone: 01223 335900
ADDRESS:	Free to visit.
VISITING:	Check with the Porter's Lodge for visiting times.

29. CLARE HALL — FOUNDED IN 1966

INFO:	Clare Hall has the highest fellow to student ratio within the University.
SIZE:	145 graduate students.
ALUMNI:	Dr Phyllis Starkey (MP)
ADDRESS:	Herschel Road, CB3 9AL. Telephone: 01223 332360
VISITING:	Normally closed to visitors.

30. HOMERTON COLLEGE — FOUNDED IN 1976

INFO:	The University's College of Education, specialising in degrees in teacher training.
SIZE:	600 undergraduates and 600 graduate students.
ALUMNI:	Nick Hancock (comedian and presenter), Cherie Lunghi (actress) and Jan Ravens (actress and impressionist)
ADDRESS:	Hills Road, Cambridge, CB2 8PH. Telephone: 01223 507111
VISITING:	Normally closed to visitors. Visits may be possible by prior arrangement. Contact the Porter's Lodge for details.

31. ROBINSON COLLEGE — FOUNDED IN 1981

INFO:	Founded by Sir David Robinson. His donation of £17 million is the largest single gift in the history of the University.
SIZE:	397 undergraduates and 105 graduates.
ALUMNI:	Nick Clegg (MP), Konnie Huq (TV presenter) and Robert Webb (comedian and writer).
ADDRESS:	Grange Road, CB3 9AN. Telephone: 01223 339100.
VISITING:	Normally closed to visitors. Visits may be possible by prior arrangement. Contact the Porter's Lodge for details.

THE FIRST UNIVERSITY TIDDLYWINKS SOCIETY WAS FORMED IN CAMBRIDGE IN 1955.

King's College Chapel
A Cambridge icon

One of the most visually recognisable buildings in the world, King's College Chapel is a truly incredible building.

The chapel was the brainchild of Henry VI who was just 19 years old when, in 1441, he laid the foundation stone of the college. Henry was famed for his love of architecture and religion and his first concern was to build a fitting chapel for the college. Work began in 1446. Just nine years later, the War of the Roses broke out in England and work on the chapel was severely hampered, first by a lack of money and then by Henry's imprisonment and eventual execution by the new King, Edward IV.

It was not until the reign of Richard III that work began again on the chapel. In 1485, at the battle of Bosworth, Richard was killed in battle by Henry VII. Henry devoted himself to continuing work on the chapel in honour of his uncle, Henry VI.

During Henry VIII's reign, the windows and much of the woodwork were installed. By the time of his death in 1547, and after witnessing the reign of no fewer than five monarchs, the chapel was finally complete.

This beautiful building bears the marks of each of its royal contributors and the turbulent history during its construction. The interior vaulting of the chapel is decorated with intricately carved coats of arms and Tudor motifs. Look closely at the beautiful oak screen, which stands between the antechapel and the choir. On it, the initials of Henry VIII and his then bride Anne Boleyn are entwined. Rubens' striking painting 'Adoration of the Magi' stands above the high altar.

A Festival of Nine Lessons and Carols is held every year on Christmas Eve in the chapel. The service was first played on the radio in 1928 and is now broadcast to millions of people around the world. People queue for hours on Christmas Eve to get tickets to this hugely popular event.

Open to visitors:

Term time: 09.30 - 15.30 Monday to Friday, 09.30 - 15.15 Saturday and 13.15 - 14.15 Sunday.
Out of term: 09.30 - 16.30 Monday to Saturday and 10.00 - 17.00 Sunday.

Admission: Adults, £4.50, children, students and senior citizens, £3. Children under 12 are free of charge when visiting with their family.

THE CHAPEL HAS ONE OF THE FINEST EXAMPLES OF A FAN VAULTED CEILING IN THE WORLD.

Cambridge Museums
Expect the unexpected

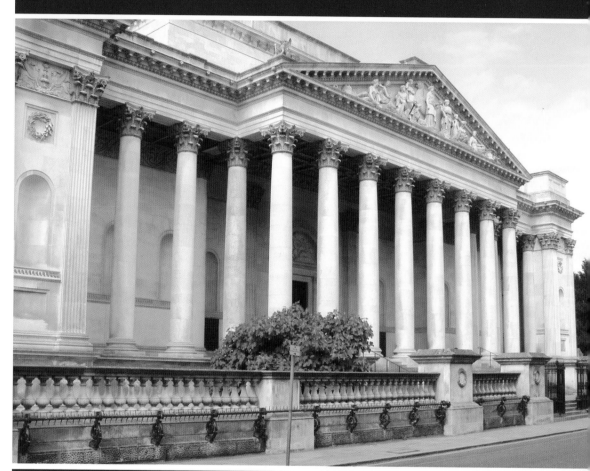

THE FITZWILLIAM MUSEUM

The Fitzwilliam Museum is the art museum of the University and houses collections of works of art and antiquities spanning centuries and civilisations. The museum was opened in its present location in 1848. The magnificent Founder's Building (pictured above) was designed by George Basevi. As well as works by artists such as Constable, Monet and Picasso, there are also artefacts from Ancient Greece and Rome on display. The museum is also home to one of the UK's finest collections of exhibits from Ancient Egypt.

Opening Times
OPEN: Tuesday-Saturday: 10:00-17:00
Sunday and Bank Holiday Mondays:: 12:00-17:00
CLOSED: Mondays, Good Friday and 24-26 & 31 December and 1 January

Free Admission
Address: Trumpington Street, Cambridge CB2 1RB
Telephone: 01223 332900
Website: www.fitzmuseum.cam.ac.uk

CAMBRIDGE'S CREST SHOWS THE RIVER AND 3 SHIPS INDICATING THE CITY'S HISTORY AS A PORT.

THE ZOOLOGY MUSEUM

e University Museum of Zoology houses a
cinating collection of zoological exhibits, including
veral specimens collected during Darwin's famous
yage onboard The Beagle.

plays include everything from the tiniest fossils to
e huge skeleton of a finback whale, found washed
ore on the Sussex coastline in 1865. The
leton has become the symbol for the museum and
ngs outside the main entrance.

Opening Times
OPEN: Monday - Friday 10.00 - 16.45
CLOSED: Weekends and Bank Holidays.

Free Admission
Address: Downing Street, Cambridge, CB2 3EJ
Telephone: 01223 336650
Website: www.zoo.cam.ac.uk

THE WHIPPLE MUSEUM

The Whipple Museum holds an important collection of
scientific instruments and models dating from the Middle
Ages to the present day.

The Museum was founded in 1944 by Robert Whipple.
Whipple worked as an assistant to Darwin's youngest son,
Horace, the founder of the Cambridge Scientific
Instrument Company. Whipple went on to become the
chairman of the company and over the course of his life,
amassed a collection of over 1000 scientific instruments.
This fascinating collection forms the basis of the museum.

Opening Times
OPEN: Monday - Friday 12.30 - 16.30
CLOSED: Weekends and Bank Holidays (opening
times can vary, please check in advance)

Free Admission
Address: Free School Lane, Cambridge, CB2 3RH
Telephone: 01223 330906
Website: www.hps.cam.ac.uk/whipple

THE SEDGWICK MUSEUM OF EARTH SCIENCES

The Sedgwick Museum takes visitors on a journey through more than 500 million years of the history of life on Earth. Giant marine reptiles, dinosaurs and a 125,000 year old hippo found in Cambridgeshire are among the fascinating collection of exhibits.

Opening Times
OPEN: Monday to Friday, 10.00 - 13.00 and 14.00 - 17.00, Saturday 10.00 - 16.00.
CLOSED: Sundays and Bank Holidays

Free Admission
Address: Downing Street, Cambridge CB2 3EQ
Telephone: 01223 333456
Website: www.sedgwickmuseum.org

ARCHAEOLOGY & ANTHROPOLOGY

Explore the fascinating collections of artefacts from peoples and cultures around the world. Museum highlights include material collected on Captain Cook's voyages of exploration and a 14-metre high totem pole from Canada. Find out about archaeology in the Archaeology Galleries, including painted pottery from Peru, gilded Anglo Saxon brooches and Roman altar stones.

Opening Times
OPEN: Tuesday-Saturday 10.30-16.30
CLOSED: Sundays and Bank Holidays

Free Admission
Address: Downing Street, Cambridge CB2 3DZ
Telephone: 01223 333516
Website: www.maa.cam.ac.uk

MUSEUM OF CLASSICAL ARCHAEOLOGY

Often referred to as 'The Ark', the museum is one of Cambridge's hidden gems.

The museum houses one of the largest collections of plaster casts of Greek and Roman statues in the world.

Opening Times
OPEN: Monday to Friday 10.00 - 17.00, Saturdays 10.00 - 13.00
CLOSED: Sundays and Bank Holidays

Free Admission
Address: Sidgwick Avenue, Cambridge CB3 9DA
Telephone: 01223 335153
Website: www.classics.cam.ac.uk/museum

SCOTT POLAR RESEARCH INSTITUTE

Founded in 1920 as the national memorial to Captain RF Scott and his companions who perished on their return from the South Pole, this museum houses collections on all aspects of polar exploration. The fascinating exhibits range from penguins to skidoos, Inuit art to explorers' diaries of Antarctic expeditions, sledges, equipment, photographs and much more.

Opening Times
OPEN: Tuesday-Friday 11-13.00 and 14.00 - 16.00, Saturday 12 - 16.00
CLOSED: Sundays, Mondays and Bank Holidays

Free Admission
Address: Lensfield Road, Cambridge CB2 1ER
Telephone: 01223 336540
Web: www.spri.cam.ac.uk/museum

BOTANIC GARDEN

e Botanic Garden is a nquil 40-acre (16 :tares) garden which ers year round interest to tors. The Garden has a ection of over 8,000 nt species in beautifully dscaped settings, including : Rock Garden, Lake, isshouses, Winter Garden, oodland Walk, and nine tional Collections.

Opening Times
PEN: Daily, 10.00 - 18.00 April to September, 10.00 - 7.00 February, March and October and 10.00- 16.00 ovember to January.
4.00 for adults 17 - 60. £3.50 for adults over 60 and tudents in possession of a recognised student card. hildren under 16 are admitted free. (Children must be ccompanied by an adult at all times).
ddress: 1 Brookside, Cambridge, CB2 1JE
elephone: 01223 336265
Vebsite: www.botanic.cam.ac.uk

KETTLE'S YARD

Kettle's Yard is the beautiful former home of Jim Ede, once a curator at the Tate Gallery. It houses a collection of 20th C Century art including works by Henry Moore, Barbara Hepworth, Alfred Wallis, Ben and Winifred Nicholson, Christopher Wood and Henri Gaudier-Breszka. Next door is a gallery that presents contemporary and modern art exhibitions.

Opening Times
OPEN: Tuesday-Sunday and Bank Holiday Mondays 14.00 — 16.00 (winter), Tuesday-Sunday and Bank Holiday Mondays 13.30 — 16.30 (April to September).CLOSED: Mondays, Good Friday, 24-26 December, 29 December and 1 January.

Free Admission
Address: Castle Street, Cambridge CB3 0AQ
Telephone: 01223 748100
Website: www.kettlesyard.co.uk

WREN LIBRARY

nity College's Wren Library is completed in 1695 to the sign of Sir Christopher ren. Among the special lections are 1250 medieval anuscripts; the Capell lection of early Shakespeare tions; many books from Sir ac Newton's own library and A. Milne's manuscripts of innie-the-Pooh and The ouse at Pooh Corner.

Opening Times
PEN: Monday - Friday, 12.00 - 14.00, Saturday, 10.30 - 2.30. NB. Opening times may vary according to term dates.
LOSED: Sundays and Bank Holidays.
ee admission for entry to library only via Queen's Road ntrance (charge for grounds applies via Trinity College reat Gate). Only 15 visitors allowed at any one time.
ddress: Trinity College, Cambridge, CB2 1TQ
elephone: 01223 338400
Vebsite: www.trin.cam.ac.uk

CAMBRIDGE FOLK MUSEUM

Housed in a former 16th Century inn, the museum tells the story of centuries of local life and folklore in Cambridge and the surrounding area.

Exhibits include inventive and often unsavoury ancient remedies for an array of ailments and an ingenious contraption for trapping bed bugs!

Opening Times
OPEN: Tuesday to Saturday 10.30 - 17.00, Sunday 14.00 - 17.00;
CLOSED: Mondays (except Bank Holidays)

Adults £3.50, Concessions £2, Children £1,.
Note: 1 free child ticket with every full paying adult.

Address: 2 - 3 Castle Street, Cambridge, CB3 0AQ
Telephone: 01223 355159
Website: www.folkmuseum.org.uk

THE UNIVERSITY LIBRARY HOLDS OVER 7 MILLION BOOKS AND 1 MILLION MAPS.

Did you know..?

Surprising Stories

✗ TRAIL BLAZERS

The scarlet jackets worn by the St John's Lady Margaret Boat Club crew are the origin of the word 'blazer' now used to describe a brightly coloured sports jacket.

Lady Margaret Boat Club Blazer

✗ OUT OF HARM'S WAY

Cambridge Train Statio

Cambridge railway station has the third longest platform in the UK. In the 19th Century, the University blocked plans to build a station within the city centre as it was concerned that students would be tempted away from their studies by the bright lights of London.

✗ RULES ARE RULES

Football has been popular in Cambridge since the 16th Century however it was in 1848 that the city really made its mark on the game with the defining of 'The Cambridge Rules'. Until this date, confusion had reigned during matches as players each followed the rules of his former school.

To put an end to the often violent disputes that resulted, a committee of 14 men, representing the various public and non public schools, met to draw up a definitive list of rules. These rules allowed no hacking, tripping or handling of the ball. As the committee decreed, it would be the triumph of 'skill over force'. The Cambridge Rules formed the basis of those set out by the modern Football Association (FA).

Parker's Piece

✗ TRINITY PETS

Sir Isaac Newton is believed to have invented the cat flap whilst studying at Trinity College. Although pets were not strictly permitted at the college, a blind eye was turned to those who kept cats, since they helped keep the mice and rat population down. Poet Lord Byron joined Trinity in 1805. Apparently, in protest at college rules that dogs were not permitted, animal lover Byron instead acquired a pet bear! He kept the bear in his college rooms a took it for walks around the grounds.

✗ THE ACCLAIMED CAMBRIDGE FOLK FESTIVAL IS HELD EVERY AUGUST IN CHERRY HINTON HALL

NOSEY PARKER

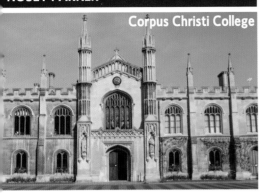
Corpus Christi College

e term Nosey Parker is thought to originate from 16th Century master of Corpus Christi College, tthew Parker. He founded the Corpus Christi ary in the 1560s and amassed a collection of 600 nuscripts and 20,000 printed books. Parker velled the length and breadth of the country to ff out' additions to the collection, thus earning self the nickname 'Nosey'.

WOODEN SPOON

e term Wooden Spoon originates from Cambridge versity. From at least the early 19th Century, a oden spoon was presented to the student who l achieved the lowest pass mark in the athematical Tripos.

e spoon, sometimes as large as 1.5 metres in gth was dangled from the balcony of the Senate use as the poor individual in question received his gree from the Vice Chancellor.

thbert Lempriere Holthouse was the last person to eive the wooden spoon in 1909. After this date, ults were given in alphabetical order, making it oossible to tell who had received the lowest mark.

MAY BALLS IN JUNE

NIGHT CLIMBERS

Senate House Leap

Night Climbing is a Cambridge tradition dating back to the 1890s. Members of the clandestine club would climb college buildings such as The Senate House, the spires of King's College Chapel and St John's Chapel under the cover of darkness. A book published in the 1930s 'The Nightclimbers of Cambridge' details the climbing routes followed with accompanying photos. The book is published under the pseudonym 'Whipplesnaith' in accordance with the secretive nature of the group.

THE MASTER CRICKETER

Hobbs Pavilion

The Hobbs Pavilion on Parker's Piece is a tribute to Cambridge boy and legendary cricketer, Jack Hobbs (1882 - 1963). Hobbs' father was a member of staff at the nearby Fenner's cricket ground and as a young boy Jack was inspired to take up the game. As a batsman, 'The Master' as he was known, scored more runs and more centuries in first class cricket than any other player in the history of the game.

Traditionally, college balls were held in May, some two weeks before the start of exams. In more recent times the date has sensibly been shifted to the end of the exam period in mid June. May Balls are lavish affairs with tickets to the biggest (St. John's and Trinity) often exceeding £120 each. The eating, drinking and dancing carries on throughout the night and into the following morning. Those hardy enough to last the distance pose for the 'survivors' photo' taken at around 6am.

10 THINGS
YOU MUST DO IN
Cambridge

1. CLIMB GT. ST. MARY'S CHURCH TOWER

In this famously flat landscape, the tower is one of the only places from which you can get a good view of the city and surrounding area. On a clear day, it is even possible to see Ely Cathedral, some 16 miles away. There are 123 spiralling steps in the confined tower, so pace yourself!

Address: Senate House Hill, Cambridge, CB2 3PQ
Telephone: 01223 741716
Website: www.gsm.cam.ac.uk

2. MESS ABOUT ON THE RIVER

No visit to Cambridge is complete without a trip on the River Cam.

Whether you're feeling brave enough to punt yourself or prefer to take the more leisurely option of a chauffeured trip, you are sure to enjoy the beautiful 'Backs'.

Punt trips available from Mill Lane and Quayside.
Scudamores Punting Company
Tel: 01223 359750

3. TAKE TEA AT THE ORCHARD

Enjoy the Great British tradition of afternoon tea in the glorious surroundings of The Orchard Tearoooms in Grantchester. It was a favourite meeting place of 'The Grantchester Group', including poet Rupert Brooke, who lived at the Old Vicarage. He is remembered in the small museum at the Tearooms.

Address: 45 - 47 Mill Way, Grantchester, CB3 9ND
Telephone: 01223 845788
Website: www.orchard-grantchester.com

4. HIRE A BIKE

Join the thousands of students and residents who know that the best way to travel around Cambridge is by bike. With dedicated cycle lanes and suggested routes to follow, get out in the open air and explore the pretty Cambridgeshire villages and countryside.

Cycle hire from £6 per half day available from:
City Cycle Hire Ltd.
Tel.: 01223 365629

CAMBRIDGE IS TWINNED WITH HEIDELBERG IN GERMANY AND SZEGED IN HUNGARY.

5. VISIT KING'S COLLEGE CHAPEL

g's College Chapel
k over 100 years to
d and was finally
npleted in 1547. The
erior vaulting of the
pel is decorated with
icately carved Tudor
tifs. Rubens' striking
nting 'Adoration of
Magi' stands above
high altar.

ddress: King's College, Cambridge, CB2 1ST.
lephone: 01223 331100
ebsite: www.kings.cam.ac.uk

6. WHALE WATCHING AT ZOOLOGY MUSEUM

The Zoology Museum houses
an extensive collection of
scientifically important
zoological exhibits including
many specimens collected by
Charles Darwin. The entrance
to the museum is presided
over by the enormous
skeleton of a Finback Whale
which was washed ashore off
the coast of Sussex in 1865.

Address: New Museums Site, Cambridge, CB2 3EJ.
Telephone: 01223 336650
Website: www.zoo.cam.ac.uk/museum/

7. VISIT A CAMBRIDGE COLLEGE

th 31 colleges to
ose from, there are
nty of opportunities to
k into the world of the
iversity. Most colleges
open to visitors, with
exception of exam
iods. Our college list
details of opening
es and any applicable
mission charges.

ddress: Various
elephone: Various
Vebsite: www.cam.ac.uk

8. PLANE SPOTTING AT DUXFORD

Located just 10 miles South
of Cambridge, Duxford
Imperial War Museum is
Europe's premier aviation
museum. The museum
houses the finest collections
of tanks, military vehicles and
naval exhibits in the country
and hosts several spectacular
air shows throughout the
year.

A regular bus service (C7) operates daily between
Cambridge bus station and the Museum.
Telephone: 01223 835000

9. CHELSEA BUNS AT FITZBILLIES

zbillies was established
1922 and became a
mbridge landmark.
orld famous for its
icious Chelsea Buns
ade to a fiercely
arded secret recipe),
tea room is the ideal
ce to treat yourself.
nch and dinner are also
ved daily.

ddress: 52 Trumpington Street, CB2 1RG
elephone: 01223 352500
Vebsite: www.fitzbillies.co.uk

10. BOTANIC GARDEN FLORA AND FAUNA

The Cambridge University
Botanic Garden displays over
8,000 different plant species
in 40 acres of beautiful
landscapes. Located on
Trumpington Road, just 1 mile
from the city centre, the
Garden is a wonderful place
to explore at your leisure.

Address: 1 Brookside, Cambridge, CB2 1JE
Telephone.: 01223 336265
Website: www.botanic.cam.ac.uk

CAMBRIDGE INHABITANTS REFER TO OXFORD (THEIR ARCH RIVAL) AS 'THE OTHER PLACE'.

Live The City Quiz

The finale to your trail

Did you solve all the clues?

For each of the three trails, we have created a fun, multiple-choice quiz for you to play to see how many clues you solved correctly. It is **FREE** to play and best of all you could be a winner in our competition prize draw.

How to play the quiz

1 The page on your right contains your unique quiz code. Have this with you when you are ready to play.

2 Go to our website at **www.livethecity.com** and click on 'Play The Quiz'.

3 Enter your quiz code when prompted and then follow the on-screen instruction to start.

✽ The Competition Prize Draw

For the chance to win one of five **£100** cash prizes simply enter your details at the end of the quiz.

- ✽ Your quiz code entitles you to play each Cambridge quiz once.
- ✽ For every correct answer, you'll earn one entry into our competition prize draw.
- ✽ The more you score, the more chances you have of winning.
- ✽ Score maximum points in all 3 quizzes and you'll receive 52 draw entries in total!
- ✽ Draw dates, prize details and full terms and conditions are available on our website.

... Best of luck.